PRAISE FOR CHRISTIAN S. KELSO and
BUILDING YOUR CASTLE

"Everyone has heard a story of how a family came to blows over a contested inheritance. Christian Kelso's book helps you avoid this kind of family tragedy."

~ Beck Weathers, M.D., Climber & Author

"Families need teamwork, engagement, and cultural identity just like businesses do. Christian's techniques teach families to develop these skills just like my coaching does for business leaders."

~ Jason Treu, Chief People Officer and Executive Coach

"This book is a fantastic resource for navigating rough waters between family members when life and law collide."

~ Jeremy Anderson, Family Lawyer and Cast Member of ABC's The Bachelorette

"Christian does a great job of making complex legal concepts easy to understand!"

~ Orly Mazur, Professor of Taxation, SMU Dedman School of Law

"A must read for adult children and their ageing parents. Very well written, easy to follow despite being a heady subject. Truly wish I had this book as a guideline for conversation with my father before he passed. I could have made things much easier for the family."

~ Dr. Alisa Rich, CEO of Wipe Out Kids' Cancer

Books by Christian S. Kelso

BUILDING YOUR CASTLE

NOVEL INSTINCTS PUBLISHING

Santa Fe | Dallas

NovelInstincts.com

Copyright © 2019 by Christian S. Kelso. This book, or parts thereof,
may not be reproduced in any form (print or digital) without the permission
of the author.

This publication contains the opinions and the ideas of the author. It is sold with the understanding that neither the author nor the publisher is engaged in rendering legal, tax, investment, insurance, financial, accounting or other professional advice or services. If the reader requires those services, a competent professional should be consulted. Relevant laws vary from state to state. The strategies outlined in this book may not be suitable for every individual and are not guaranteed or warranted to produce any particular results. No warranty is made with respect to the accuracy or completeness of the information contained herein, and both the author and the publisher specifically DISCLAIM any responsibility for any liability, loss, or risk, personal or otherwise, which is incurred as a consequence, directly or indirectly, of the use and application of any of the contents of this book.

Mr. Kelso is available for live events. Please contact him through his website: ChristianKelso.com

ISBN: 978-1-7923-1731-6

1. Educational / Guidance / Financial Planning / Law

Library of Congress Control Number: 20199116813

Printed in the United States of America.

10 9 8 7 6 5 4 3 2 1

This book's text is composed in the font Calibri Regular at 11 point.

Its page numbers and chapter heads are in DIN Regular and Bold Condensed

BUILDING YOUR CASTLE

A practical guide for protecting your legacy.

Christian S. Kelso, Esq.

NOVEL INSTINCTS
Publishers of fine genre fiction and non-fiction.

Christian S. Kelso, Esq. is a Dallas attorney practicing in the areas of estate planning, wealth preservation and transfer, probate, tax, and transactional corporate law. He has counseled both the rich and famous and the not so famous. His approach is simple: Find practical, cost-effective solutions that avoid costly, and often heartbreaking disputes in both the courtroom and the living room. Throughout his career, Christian has been dedicated to making the law work for his clients and their families.

A native of Dallas, Christian attended both St. Mark's School of Texas and the University of Texas, then earned both his J.D. and his LL.M. in taxation from Southern Methodist University. Christian now lives in North Texas and is active in the community, sitting on charitable boards and other governing bodies. He speaks German and Spanish fluently, and enjoys traveling the world with his wife and two children.

Acknowledgements This book would never have come together without the help of a rather large group of people, and they all have my utmost gratitude and thanks. First, thank you to everyone who took the time to read my manuscripts and provide feedback, especially those who are quoted in the opening pages and on its covers. Thanks to Kristy Elam and Katherine Coleman for their eagle-eyed proofing skills. Thanks also to Bridget Boland of Modern Muse for editing and structural guidance. Paul Black of Paul Black Design deserves thanks for many of the technical aspects of the book, including the cover art and internal design. Paul also gets credit for spending Sundays listening to me and putting up with my nit-picky changes of countless details. I am thankful to Liza Farrow-Gillespie for her technical advice about publishing and for being a sounding board on several occasions. Thanks to Martha Newman for motivating me to get this project underway. Most importantly, of course, thank you to my wife, Bethany, and the rest of my family for putting up with me. This book has been a dream of mine for years and I was only able to pull it off with your gracious support, kindness, encouragement, tolerance, and understanding. Thank you all!

TABLE OF CONTENTS

1 Laying the Groundwork. 1
   1.1   Introduction. 1
   1.2   Some Problems. 5
      1.2.1   The Family Power Vacuum............................... 5
      1.2.2   Daddy Loved Me More...................................... 10
      1.2.3   Wicked Stepmother/Greedy Stepchildren. 14
      1.2.4   Head in the Sand. 16
      1.2.5   No One is Immune. 17
   1.3   Benefits. 19
      1.3.1   Prevent the Family Power Vacuum................... 19
      1.3.2   Let the Air in Slowly. 19
      1.3.3   Enjoy the Fruits. 23
      1.3.4   Watch and Learn; Guide and Grow. 25
2 The Toolbox 27
   2.1   Generally. 27
   2.2   Professionals. 28
      2.2.1   Attorneys. 30
      2.2.2   Investment Managers and Insurance Brokers. . 31
      2.2.3   Care Managers. 32
      2.2.4   CPAs. 34

	2.2.5	Genealogists.	35
	2.2.6	Appraisers.	35
	2.2.7	Facilitators.	37
	2.2.8	Trustees.	38
2.3		Family Assembly.	40
2.4		Family Mission Statement.	41
2.5		Family Constitution.	44
	2.5.1	Decision-making.	45
	2.5.2	Identification.	46
	2.5.3	Enfranchisement.	46
	2.5.4	Dispute resolution.	46
	2.5.5	Stewardship.	46
	2.5.6	Appointments.	47
	2.5.7	Meetings.	47
	2.5.8	Amendments.	47
	2.5.9	Consequences.	47
	2.5.10	Emergency Procedures.	48
	2.5.11	Divorce.	48
	2.5.12	Respect.	48
	2.5.13	Religion/Morals/Values.	48
	2.5.14	Care for Elderly.	49
	2.5.15	Exclusivity.	49
	2.5.16	Departure.	49
	2.5.17	Holidays.	49
2.6		Family History Narrative.	50
2.7		Family Counsel.	52
2.8		Committees.	52
2.9		Comprehensive Estate Plan.	53
2.10		Trusts.	56
2.11		Guardianship.	57
2.12		Asset Protection Plans.	59
2.13		Life Insurance.	61
2.14		Intra-Family Loans.	62
2.15		Gifts.	64
3		Recognizing and Leveraging Various Family Personalities.	67
	3.1	The Lord as Project Manager.	67
	3.2	Acceptance as a First Step.	69

- 3.3 Enfranchisement. 71
  - 3.3.1 Who to Enfranchise? 72
  - 3.3.2 When to Enfranchise? 72
  - 3.3.3 How to Enfranchise? 74
  - 3.3.4 Why Enfranchise? 75
- 3.4 Communication. 76
  - 3.4.1 Misinterpretation. 79
- 3.5 The Mad Hatters. 82
  - 3.5.1 Patriarch. 82
  - 3.5.2 Coastal. 85
  - 3.5.3 Cassandra. 89
  - 3.5.4 Eldest Son. 91
  - 3.5.5 The Wanderer. 93
  - 3.5.6 Black Sheep. 96
  - 3.5.7 Caregiver/Responsible Party. 104
  - 3.5.8 Fiduciary. 107
  - 3.5.9 Stepmothers. 110
  - 3.5.10 Sheriff. 112
- 3.6 Children & Grandchildren: 113
  - 3.6.1 The Uninitiated Generation. 114
  - 3.6.2 The Skip Generation. 117
- 4 Dealing with Dilemmas of Contingency Planning 121
  - 4.1 The Inevitable and the Not So Inevitable. 121
  - 4.2 Wills. 124
    - 4.2.1 Disposition of Probate Property. 125
    - 4.2.2 Executor Appointment. 126
    - 4.2.3 Manner of Disposition. 127
    - 4.2.4 Exercise Powers of Appointment. 128
  - 4.3 Trusts. 130
    - 4.3.1 Probate Avoidance. 130
    - 4.3.2 Incapacity. 131
    - 4.3.3 Real Property in Another State. 133
    - 4.3.4 Privacy and Security. 133
    - 4.3.5 Continuity of Business Management. 134
  - 4.4 Durable Power of Attorney. 135
  - 4.5 Guardianship. 136
- 5 Timing Issues. 138

5.1	Chronos & Kairos.	138
5.2	Family Assemblies.	139
5.3	Enfranchisement.	143
5.3.1	Talking to Children About Money.	145
5.3.2	Talking to Sons- and Daughters-In-Law About Money.	150
5.4	Talking to Patriarchs About Money.	152
5.5	Talking to Trustees About Money.	155
5.6	When to cut the cord.	157
6	The Program: A Blueprint for Your Family Assembly.	160
6.1	The Cornerstone.	160
6.2	Planning and Preparation.	161
6.3	Comprehensive Family Assembly Program.	164
6.3.1	Module 1: Discuss Family Lore.	164
6.3.2	Module 2: Review Family Mission Statement.	167
6.3.3	Module 3: Status Update.	170
6.3.4	Module 4: Set Goals.	175
6.3.5	Module 5: Plan of Attack.	177
6.3.6	Module 6: Take Stock.	179
6.3.7	Module 7: Celebrate.	180
6.4	Additional Modules.	180
6.4.1	Run Scenarios.	180
6.4.2	Third Party Narrative.	183
6.4.3	Educational Modules.	184
6.4.4	"Spotlight."	185
6.4.5	Kids' Presentation.	185
6.4.6	Enfranchisement Ceremonies.	185
6.4.7	Committee Meetings.	186
6.4.8	Grievance Hearings.	186
6.4.9	Planning Future Assemblies.	187
6.4.10	Elections.	187
6.4.11	Family Photographs.	187
6.4.12	Blind Evaluations.	187
7	Tips & Tricks from the Trenches	190
7.1	Flexibility.	190
7.2	Play the Long Ball.	191
7.3	Eyes on the Prize.	191

7.4	Don't Keep Score.		192
7.5	Fairness.		194
7.6	Live in Sin (to Avoid Blended Families).		195
7.7	Don't Give Up on Anyone.		197
7.8	Taking the Keys.		198
7.9	Rules of Family Decorum.		202
	7.9.1	The Golden Rule.	202
	7.9.2	Say "Thank You" (and Mean It).	203
	7.9.3	Lincoln's Unsent Letters.	203
	7.9.4	Atticus' Rule.	204
7.10	Crowd Surfing.		205
7.11	Have Fun.		206

LAYING THE GROUNDWORK

1.1 Introduction.

I sometimes joke that my trial lawyer friends drive sports cars and wear expensive Italian suits, while I roll my sleeves up and go to work every day. I did not go to law school to be a litigator. Most lawyers help clients get out of trouble. I help clients avoid trouble in the first place.

As an attorney focused on estate planning and wealth preservation, I've noticed a few things others seem to ignore. Families that successfully manage and transfer their wealth have something in common. It's not just high-quality estate planning. Many families that are *unsuccessful* at managing and transferring wealth have very good estate planning, so the ones that get it right must have something more going for them. Instead, what seems to differentiate the success stories from the failures is something less tangible than a well-written Will or trust agreement. There is something else involved that seems to keep some families on track while others fall apart. The common threads present in nearly all of the successful families and absent from those that fail are effective communication and involvement between and within the family.

Wealth can be both a blessing and a curse. On the one hand, it is the lifeblood of the family, literally putting food on the table, opening doors to education, providing opportunity in business and personal relationships, and increasing the family's standard of living. On the other hand, wealth can be a destructive force. In its shadow lie some of our darkest and most powerful emotions, such as greed, fear, and jealousy. These emotions can smash into a family with astonishingly destructive power, and ultimately tear the family apart.

The cues we get from society tell us that success in life is defined in terms of the amount of wealth we are able to amass. When we have built up a fortune, we flaunt it with expensive toys and trinkets. We even use terms, like "retail therapy," which drive home the notion that spending money will make us feel good. The natural conclusion is that the more money we have, the better we feel by spending it. And yet, plenty of people who aren't wealthy are perfectly happy.

On the other hand, most truly successful people will tell you that gaining wealth is the easy part. Keeping it is much harder. Teaching our kids to keep it is harder still. Most Americans avoid the topic of wealth within the family except in unhappy and unproductive circumstances. Wealth is generally controlled and managed by a family head to the exclusion of other family members. Information flow among family members can be disparate, or at least perceived as such. Discussion of wealth, even in the family context, is considered taboo. This leaves children or other family members ill-prepared to manage a family's investments or the family business when the head steps down or dies. Not to mention the fact that the transition of family power is highly charged, emotionally.

The ultra-wealthy have a few tricks for staying wealthy. One of these tricks is that they operate their family like a business. They take the time to think about and discuss who they are as a family and what they want to accomplish. They set goals as a family and openly discuss how to reach them. They give each family member an opportunity to do what he or she can, in furtherance of the family's goals. They don't ignore the obvious or the inevitable. If something is important to discuss, they talk about it, even if it is taboo or uncomfortable. In other words, the ultra-wealthy make wealth preservation their business and they systematically go about doing what's necessary to avoid problems.

Treating a family like a business has many advantages. It allows families to prepare for problems before they occur. It allows them to recognize and leverage untapped assets they never knew they had in the form of perspectives, personalities, and the abilities of various family members. It also allows families to economize and efficiently maximize their unique potentials. When families operate like a business, they implement systems for things like training younger generations about wealth management and providing accountability for each family member's performance. Developing and implementing these systems is always time-consuming and often expensive. Various professionals usually help families do this; however, these professionals' services are effectively priced out of most families' grasp. But that doesn't mean families of more modest means can't benefit from the techniques and tools they provide.

This book is designed as a do-it-yourself guide for families to develop and implement family systems just like those the ultra-wealthy use to keep their houses in order. It's not strictly focused on financial wealth, because that is too narrowminded. Nor is this book about estate planning, although that will be discussed at length because it is integral to the overall process. This book provides an explanation of the tools available as well as the instances where each might be utilized. It also includes some anecdotal advice on how to successfully manage and transfer wealth to future generations.

This book is also about strengthening bonds between family members and leveraging the capabilities each one of them brings to the table to turn the family into a powerful, unified entity where each family member can lead a happier, more fulfilled life. In other words, it is about finding satisfaction and joy. To do this successfully, families often need to identify assets they never knew they had, and as you will see, many of these assets are not financial assets in the traditional sense. Families must then learn how to channel and harmonize their assets so they function as a constructive force to push the family towards realizing its maximum potential. Most families' greatest assets transcend traditional notions of wealth. Finally, this book identifies potential pitfalls families face and teaches how to avoid them.

In this book, we will examine the techniques used by the ultra-wealthy and adapt them to function effectively in the context of more modest wealth. Many professionals refer to the tools laid out in this book as "family systems" or "family governance," but I prefer to think of them on slightly different terms. I call it "**Building your Castle**."

Castles represent strength and permanence. They invoke romance and intrigue. Castles are also homes; in particular, they are homes to families of stature, success, and importance. On the other hand, castles also represent safety and shelter for all sorts of people.

A castle cannot be built by one person acting alone. Building a castle requires good faith collaboration from all sorts of skilled specialists as well as unskilled laborers. Every castle is unique; built to fit a particular set of needs. Nor are castles built in a day. They are assembled stone-by-stone. Many castles have been added onto over time, so the structure we see today is nothing like the original.

In many ways, these attributes mirror the successful families described in this book.

Building Your Castle is part guide book and part reference book. It is meant to serve as a guide to families as they make purposeful efforts towards goal-oriented success. For those who are already on this path, the book is also meant to serve as a reference to spark new ideas or remind you of old ones that you have forgotten about. It will also help you hone and improve the techniques you already use to achieve familial success.

Most importantly, this book offers a new perspective on family relationships. I truly hope that reading it will help you better understand your own family, that you will uncover something that you never saw before, and that you will be inspired to take action. The techniques in this book are tried and true, and I hope you find them useful.

1.2 Some Problems.

To understand why the techniques taught in this book are important, I must first explain the problems it is meant to avoid. The remainder of this chapter is dedicated to this purpose.

1.2.1 The Family Power Vacuum.

Family wealth is typically managed by a matriarch or patriarch. (To keep things simple, I refer to such person, regardless of gender, as the "**Patriarch**" in this book. Similarly, I will use the universal "he" instead of "he or she" for most of the characters in this book.) Patriarchs typically act as the lord of his or her manor. They decide what form their family wealth will take, how and when it will be doled out, and who will benefit from it.

Patriarchs generally fail to provide other family members with adequate information regarding family wealth. Sometimes, the information is incomplete. From an early age, we are taught that discussing wealth is taboo, so we tend to be vague or avoid the subject altogether, even with close family members. Other times, a Patriarch will provide incorrect details about their wealth to the family. This may be done by mistake, but there are many reasons why someone would do this intentionally. For example, Patriarchs might *overstate* their assets to:

- make loved ones feel secure
- get more attention
- feel better about themselves
- avoid appearing as if they have lost control
- avoid embarrassment.

On the other hand, Patriarchs might *understate* their wealth to:

- avoid being asked for money
- prevent future generations from feeling entitled
- avoid the leaking of personal information to unrelated parties by loose-lipped family members
- encourage a strong work ethic in prospective heirs
- defend against physical attacks and kidnapping

The concentration of power in a single person and the poor dissemination of high-quality information often causes distress in family members. Disparities in control and information increase fear and anger. Concentrating power in a single person means that everyone else in the family lacks control, which can lead to a sense of helplessness, a profoundly negative emotion. In worst case scenarios, helplessness can lead to depression and other forms of mental illness. In better scenarios, it can still lead to irrational behavior. This depression or irrational behavior, which psychologists call "learned helplessness," can stem from a deep, often subconscious, feeling of lack of control.

Poor dissemination of information can have similar effects on the conscious mind as well. Ever wonder why they put windows on airplanes? There is no reason why the passengers need to see out. Seeing out does not make passengers safer. Structurally speaking, windows are weak points in the pressurized body of a typical jet liner, so they actually make planes less safe. In fact, in 1954, two de Havilland Comets, the world's first jet liner, crashed tragically because the windows, which were poorly designed and manufactured, caused the aircraft to break up in mid-flight. And yet, every major passenger plane in service has plenty of windows for passengers to look out. Why? The answer is that the windows reduce fear by increasing the amount of information available to passengers. Because we can see out of the plane, we feel safer, so we cause less trouble for the crew and other passengers.

The example of the airplane windows illustrates a very important point: Perception trumps reality. *Feeling* safer is more important than *being* safer, at least when the increased danger is minimal.

In the typical family dynamic, the Patriarch maintains control through a variety of mechanisms. The Patriarch may deploy these mechanisms subconsciously, deliberately, or in some combination of the two. For example, many families operate in a certain way simply as a matter of historical precedent (subconscious). In other situations, family members stay in line because they have been promised money (deliberate). Sometimes guilt, which is subconscious, is a major control factor. Other times, threats, which are deliberate, are used. These and other factors can be combined in infinite ways. As long as the Patriarch is alive and competent, he or she can maintain the *status quo* and keep the family system from falling apart.

The family crisis typically comes to a head when something happens to the Patriarch. I call this the "**Family Power Vacuum**." At some point, the lord becomes unable to manage the manor. Other family members recognize they must make decisions that were previously made by the Patriarch and, just as happens in any political power vacuum, people get sucked into a void left by the departed Patriarch. If this happens with more than one member of a given family, conflict typically results as the various parties vie for control.

Complicating matters is the proximate cause of the Family Power Vacuum and its effects on the family. If dad just died, or had a stroke and moved into the nursing home, the bereft kids will be grieving. Their minds need to work through the irrational emotions that naturally come with such an event. Instead, they are trying to figure out where dad left off with the family business. Although they may think they're acting rationally, more often than not, they aren't.

The irrational behavior exhibited in the context of a Family Power Vacuum can come in many forms. It is not uncommon for one or more family members to believe that they, and they alone, can fill the Patriarch's shoes. If two or more people feel this way, the potential for conflict is obvious, but even where one person steps up (or is forced up), exclusivity can be more than merely off-putting and lead to heart-rending disputes within the family. Other common irrational behaviors include spending unwarranted amounts on legal fees, debilitating indecision, and flared tempers.

Like a great novel, the Family Power Vacuum usually comes with a twist. Often, this twist is the realization that, in fact, the family is not nearly as rich as the Patriarch led people to believe. But it can be other things too, such as the extent of one family member's dependency on the Patriarch for survival. For example, one child's "failure to launch" may be known to the other children, but not fully understood until one of them takes over the finances and finally realizes how bad things have gotten. Or the twist may be the discovery of an extramarital affair or a child that resulted from that affair.

The twist typically hits the family abruptly and powerfully. It is as if, upon the lord of the manor's death, a neighboring kingdom seizes the opportunity to invade, but when the lord's children assemble the knights needed to defend the realm, they find that the knights have no horses because the lord forgot to feed them. Very few people understand just how frequently scenarios like this play out in American courtrooms.

The twist exacerbates and adds extra negativity to an already emotionally trying time. On the one hand, all of the above issues relating to inadequate information are compounded because the family members stop trusting the information they have. Once they are misled about one thing, they worry about being misled again in the future. This causes individual family members to distrust not only the person who actually misled them, but also their other family members.

Unexpected twists also increase anxiety because they cause plans to change. A family might initially think that its Patriarch has a long-term care policy in place to cover nursing home care. But when the other family members learn that the policy has long since lapsed because the Patriarch did not keep up with the payments, adjustments will have to be made for the Patriarch's care. Either the family will have to pay out of pocket, or someone will have to personally provide the requisite care.

Finally, twists can be embarrassing. This may apply in countless circumstances, including when the family learns how little wealth the Patriarch actually controlled, or of an extramarital child. Nearly every family has skeletons in its closet or some sort of "black sheep;" however, many people feel like they are the only ones with their particular circumstances. They typically lack the perspective to understand how frequently these problems happen. Even though it is misplaced, this misconception is another significant contribution to anxiety and irrational behavior.

To sum it all up, the Family Power Vacuum is a phenomenon that arises in the presence of specific circumstances: First, control is concentrated in one Patriarch. Second, that Patriarch fails, deliberately or subconsciously, to disseminate information appropriately and effectively to other family members. Finally, the Patriarch loses control.

These factors create the Family Power Vacuum and produce irrational, destructive behavior among other family members. Furthermore, the force of the Family Power Vacuum is often exacerbated by additional twists which strengthen existing negative emotions, such as fear and confusion, while adding new ones, such as embarrassment and distrust.

1.2.2 Daddy Loved Me More.

History is replete with examples of disputes that occurred over inheritance. Shortly before his death in January of 1066, Edward the Confessor, then the childless king of England, named an earl, Harold Godwinson, to be his successor. But Edward's first cousin once removed, William of Normandy, maintained that Edward had promised him the crown. By October of that year, William had invaded England and killed Harold at the battle of Hastings. We now refer to William of Normandy as William the Conqueror (and it's worth noting that he built a lot of castles).

Consider also the divisions between Sunni and Shiite Muslims. When the prophet Mohamed died in 632 A.D., a dispute arose over his religious successor. Nearly 1500 years later, the two sides are still killing each other over this dispute.

In fact, the term "succession war" is commonly used by historians to describe the many wars throughout human history that have been fought over this very subject. In many of these conflicts, the issue has been so causally linked to the underlying dispute that the word "succession" is actually included in the common name of the war (*e.g.* The War of British Succession).

The same applies in the context of literature as well. Consider Shakespeare's *King Lear*, or Dickens' *Bleak House*. Each of these dramas centers around the Family Power Vacuum. The fact that there is an entire genre on the subject affirms the ubiquity of the problem.

Any probate attorney can regale you with horror stories he or she has witnessed firsthand. These stories typically involve protracted litigation with individuals and factions competing, at least ostensibly, over the assets of their families' estates. The battles are generally senseless from an economic standpoint. But the emotions that drive them render the litigants unable to make rational decisions, leading otherwise sensible people to incur legal and other expenses far in excess of the value of the assets they are fighting over. I call this phenomenon "**Daddy Loved Me More**." Daddy Loved Me More is not really about estate assets. It is about the emotional competitions and attachments that occur in the context of the Family Power Vacuum.

Disparity of information often plays a role, albeit in a slightly different way than with the Family Power Vacuum. We praise people when they are near and disparage them when they cannot hear us. This means that we hear our parents say only good things about us, but we hear both the good and the bad things our parents have to say about our siblings, so we naturally conclude that we are the favorite child.

In October of 1962, the United States and the Soviet Union came within a hairsbreadth of killing every human being on the planet. At the core of the Cuban Missile Crisis was a disparity of information. It started when American reconnaissance aircraft photographed ballistic missile facilities in Cuba. As tensions escalated, leadership on both sides discovered that there was no effective way to conduct quick, clear, and direct communications between Washington, D. C. and Moscow. As a direct result, the "Red Line" was set up so that leaders on both sides could quickly reach each other and, hopefully, deescalate future problems before they boiled over.

A less well-known result of the Cuban Missile Crisis was the agreement to satellite flyovers. Each side, by acknowledging and allowing the other side to conduct satellite reconnaissance of its territory, dramatically reduced the overall fear and tension felt by both sides during the Cold War. For example, when one side destroyed part of its bomber fleet pursuant to arms reduction deals, the terms of the deal would typically prescribe the specific way in which each aircraft was to be destroyed and the pieces laid out. The pieces would then be left for a specified number of days to give the other side's satellites time to fly over and get a good picture. By implementing a process of systematically disseminating information, the two sides were able to avoid war. The same phenomenon applies in the context of the Family Power Vacuum and Daddy Loved Me More phenomena.

The second cause for Daddy Loved Me More also involves the perception of "Daddy" in one's mind. By the time Daddy Loved Me More manifests itself, Daddy has died. All that remains is the memory of what Daddy was, and memories are personal to each of us. Every one of Daddy's children carries with him or her a different memory and perspective of their father. The more these manifestations differ, the more likely conflict will result. The Daddy that Susie remembers actually did love Susie more than her brother, Bobby, but at the same time, the Daddy that Bobby remembers loved him more than Susie. This creates a quantum-like situation where two mutually exclusive conditions are present at the same time. If the crux of the battle between Susie and Bobby is determining or demonstrating who Daddy loved more, both Susie and Bobby will fight to the bitter end because they both know they are right.

Third, Daddy is not available to settle the dispute between the siblings. Patriarchs often fill the role of mediator, arbiter, or judge. The power to pass judgement is a particularly powerful force that adds potential energy to the Family Power Vacuum. The inability to effectively and promptly vest this power in a successor will often lead to breakdown within the family.

Fourth, love is a priceless, universal desire of every healthy human being. When the Family Power Vacuum hits, the most important source of love—the Patriarch's—is necessarily gone forever. All that remains is the memory of that love, which most of us feel should be honored and adored. But the emotional competition between family members in the contest of Daddy Loved Me More represents a direct affront, if not an outright threat, to that honoring and adoration. Many people will spend every last dollar they have proving to the world that Daddy did, in fact, Love Them More. Sadly, in the context of the Family Power Vacuum, most of us will forget that, as the Beatles put it, "money can't buy me love."

Finally, in the context of Daddy Loved Me More, there is only one conclusion. A family member's thought process goes something like this: "If Daddy really did love me more—which he clearly did—then Daddy also wanted me to have [insert anything you like here.] Daddy didn't want you to get it. He wanted me to have it, and I need that thing now, not later."

Family members often fall into this emotional trap long before Daddy dies, so they feel like they have taken ownership of one or more things long before it is proper to do so. Daddy Loved Me More makes it easy to see inheritance as a forgone conclusion rather than a windfall. Those who fall into this trap fail to understand that their interest in the Patriarch's assets is, at best, a mere expectancy. Thus, from the family member's perspective, when someone else threatens or contests that inheritance after the Patriarch has died, he or she feels as if something has been affirmatively taken away from them. When people steal from us, we naturally want to punish them. In this case, that means obtaining some sort of legal determination like a judge's order or a jury's verdict. This is an expensive prospect indeed!

1.2.3 Wicked Stepmother/Greedy Stepchildren.

Blended families have the highest rate of acrimony among their members. Probate attorneys regularly defend their clients from wicked stepmothers or greedy stepchildren, depending on which side they take, of course.

Each family member is certain that his or her opinions vis-à-vis the other are correct, making it almost impossible for either to back down or seek compromise. Forget about the fact that each side is likely working off of incomplete information because the Patriarch probably only told each family member what he or she wanted to hear, and never did so while both were present.

Most of the time, being a stepmother is a no-win scenario. When the Patriarch dies, his kids see his money as being theirs. And they want it, pronto. From her perspective, the Patriarch's good-for-nothing brats never came to visit their father until right before he died, when they could practically smell the money. This leaves her feeling resentful of them for challenging his Will and her right to his assets. Also, she needs the Patriarch's money to live on, and she believes that he wanted her to be taken care of after his death.

The children don't have it much better. They see a gold-digging harlot who is nearly their own age and never worked a day in her life. She refused to sign a prenup the Patriarch's lawyer drew up. After the Patriarch died, they might discover that everything he spent a lifetime building got moved into a joint account with the stepmother and avoided probate altogether. What did she do to deserve that?

Does any of this sound familiar? If it hasn't happened in your family, it probably has happened to someone you know. Even in those rare situations where stepchildren and stepparents get along relatively well, there is still an extra element of tension.

In all fairness to both sides, Patriarchs themselves are usually more to blame for these problems than are the kids or the stepmothers. Patriarchs want to have their cake and eat it too. They want their spouses provided for *and* they want to leave a legacy for their children. Sometimes, there just isn't enough money to go around, but they will convince themselves otherwise. Patriarchs often try to do too much with too little in the latter stages of their own lives. They overestimate their own wealth and promise the world to both sides. The don't communicate effectively with their wives or their kids, so each side is set up to be let down. And when people are let down like this, they sue.

Blended families automatically throw all the elements of the Family Power Vacuum into high gear. Can it be properly addressed? Sure. But it requires Building your Castle even stronger to withstand the extra forces at work. We will discuss how to do this later in this book.

1.2.4 Head in the Sand.

Here's a statement that estate planners hear a lot: "If my kids are dumb enough to fight over my money when I die, then they get what they deserve." We also hear things like, "What do I care what happens with my money? I'll be dead." Both of these statements indicate a level of *willful* ignorance that is almost certain to yield gut-wrenching conflict down the road.

Almost universally, the one person who should be blamed for creating a Family Power Vacuum is the one person who is no longer around. Patriarchs create Family Power Vacuums by perpetuating the circumstances that eventually lead to one. Usually, Patriarchs do this because it's easy and convenient. That is, they tell people what they want to hear, they make poor planning decisions, and they ignore hard truths because it's easier at the time. Why should they care about the children's relationships after they're gone?

Furthermore, very few Patriarchs take the hard steps needed to set their families on the right path. Instead, they stick their heads in the sand and ignore the looming problem. This is particularly frustrating because they all face the same problem. They don't each face a different problem. The problem is the same for all of them, so it is well-known, but they ignore it anyway.

Once gone, Patriarchs will never understand how much pain they have caused. They will never see the tears or the fear in their children's or spouse's eyes. They will never hear the vitriolic words their relatives scream at each other. They will never see brother turn on brother and sister turn on sister. They will be dead. This is one of the most frustrating parts of probate litigation.

1.2.5 No One is Immune.

A final problem to drive home is that no one is immune to the emotions that lead to irrational and destructive probate litigation. Lots of people think their family is special. *They* would never fight like *that* because *that's crazy*! But these are very dangerous thoughts.

When we ponder how people might react to a given set of stimuli, we almost always assume they will act rationally. Convincing ourselves to think otherwise is difficult because playing out hypothetical future events is something that only happens at the highest levels of our brains. The part of the brain that carries out our analytical thinking is almost entirely devoid of emotion. Most of the time, this is a good thing. In order to survive, we need to be able to analyze the world we are in and understand what it might do to us. The world does not operate on emotion so neither should our analytical brains, at least not most of the time.

But when emotions come into play, as they do in the Family Power Vacuum, analytical thinking stops working. The phenomenon is analogous to the worlds of Newtonian and quantum physics. The Newtonian world (named after Sir Isaac Newton who famously described gravity and many other natural phenomena) is a normal place where things act predictably. Apply so much force to such-and-such object and we can easily predict its movement. The term "quanta" was first used by physicist Max Plank to describe strange energy patterns he observed and studied. Much of Albert Einstein's work centered on quantum physics as well. In the quantum world, bizarre and unpredictable things happen, making meaningful analysis extremely difficult. The only thing one can expect is the unexpected. Thus, whereas two plus two will always equal four in the Newtonian world, in the quantum world, two plus two might equal 3 on one day and the square root of negative one on another. There is no way to tell which result you will get.

Similarly, in the context of the Family Power Vacuum, the only thing you can assume of people is that they will act irrationally. Once you take this as a given, analysis stops because there is no predictable way to move forward. All you can do is be ready to respond and adapt as necessary.

My own personal example proves the rule. When the Patriarch of my family, my grandfather, lost capacity and then eventually died, I knew the Family Power Vacuum was coming. But I thought that I would be able to act rationally and calmly throughout the process since I was a seasoned probate attorney. However, I quickly noticed that I was doing many of the irrational things I had seen my clients do. I became emotional and noticed that I was acting out on those emotions. I blamed other people for problems my grandfather should have addressed while he was alive. I fought with family members over money and acted irrationally.

My solution was to hire a probate attorney to represent me and act as a sounding board for my actions. This was one of the best decisions of my life. I understood the technical aspects of what was happening well but I also understood that my responses were irrational because I had seen my clients and their family members do many of the same things. My instruction to my attorney was narrow. I told him to watch everything I did and to keep me on a sensible path that would lead to a resolution of my family's issues in the most economical and efficient way possible. With unbiased guidance from someone who lacked the emotional baggage that always hovers around the loss of a Patriarch, I was able to diffuse the situation and come out relatively unscathed.

Merely anticipating the Family Power Vacuum is not enough to avoid its effects. You cannot simply think your way out of troubles that, by their very nature, are unpredictable and irrational. On the other hand, you can lessen or eliminate the Family Power Vacuum altogether. Later chapters in this book will show you how.

1.3 Benefits.

What benefits are available to a family that goes to the trouble of Building a Castle? One significant focus, obviously, is avoiding the family drama, protracted legal battles, expense, and heartache that tends to follow when a Patriarch dies. But there are ancillary benefits as well.

1.3.1 Prevent the Family Power Vacuum.

This book contains a number of techniques designed to help families prevent the Family Power Vacuum entirely. Most of these are based on the idea that purposeful communication among the various players will put the family in a position where the effects of Family Power Vacuum can be minimized or avoided altogether.

Although preventing the Family Power Vacuum is the ultimate goal of this book, that's not always possible. Thus, two secondary goals of this book are to mitigate the Family Power Vacuum and to protect against its impact. Mitigating the Family Power Vacuum means lessening its power. A less destructive storm is less likely to do damage to your family's Castle. Protecting against the Family Power Vacuum means Building your Castle so it is better able to withstand the storm. Fortunately, the same techniques are used to accomplish both of these goals.

1.3.2 Let the Air in Slowly.

If the Family Power Vacuum cannot be avoided in a given scenario, for example, because the Patriarch is unwilling to do the work necessary to prevent it, then the next best option is to create mechanisms to let the proverbial air back into the vacuum slowly. While this still might be a little painful, it's nothing compared to the explosive alternative.

Even though it is up to the family, not the Patriarch, to slowly let air back into the Family Power Vacuum, doing so is still every bit as much a part of Building your Castle as anything else. Building your Castle is a team effort and requires the affirmative effort of all the family members. The lord of the manor does not lay every brick in the Castle. In fact, the lord sometimes doesn't lay any of them.

If a Family Power Vacuum does occur, the natural tendency is for some force in the family—usually a strong-willed family member I will refer to in this book as the "**Sheriff**"—to rush in and attempt to fill the space that the Patriarch left behind. Usually, the Sheriff will act autonomously and have, at least in his own mind, some excuse for why he is the "right person" to take over all of the functions that the Patriarch used to do. The Sheriff usually fails, however, to fully grasp two important concepts. First, he is not the former Patriarch. He will have a different skillset and outlook on life, which means that he is probably not perfectly suited to take over all of the Patriarch's responsibilities. It's easy to armchair quarterback a Patriarch's actions, but most people find that the work is much harder than they realized. Indeed, the Patriarch's ability to make doing what they do look so easy is probably a major reason that person was the family Patriarch.

Second, the Sheriff's act of unilaterally rushing in to fill the Patriarch's space will almost always cause resentment among other family members who will feel disenfranchised because they were not consulted. Many will find the experience jarring because they perceive it as moving too quickly. Jarring experiences can lead to irrational behavior by inducing fear or by creating a sense of superiority. Other family members might look on the one who has swooped in and think, "Only my brother is barbaric enough to act like *that*!" Some family members may be caught off guard because their expectations, even irrational ones, are not met. Others may be anxious over a large physical or geographical separation. When stepping into a Patriarch's shoes, a Sheriff will often downplay or ignore the resentment that tends to build in the minds of the other family members.

On the other hand, if family members collaborate to Build a Castle, they will likely discover two very important things. First, because the Patriarch was a unique individual, it is unlikely that any one family member possesses an adequately similar skillset. Therefore, expecting that any one family member will be able to carry out all the Patriarch's duties as well as the Patriarch did is unreasonable.

A textbook example of this can be summed up as taking care of Mama and Mama's money. Assume Mama has two children. One is a wealth manager in a far-away city with little medical knowledge while the other is a nurse living near to Mama, but with low financial acumen. One day, Mama has a stroke. After that, the children have to take care of Mama and manage Mama's money. Before Mama's stroke, her relevant skillset was unique. She was the best person in the world at taking care of herself, and she was the best person in the world at managing her assets. Now that she has had a stroke, however, she is not very good at either of those things. If the wealth manager child steps into Mama's shoes, Mama's money might be well-managed, but Mama may not receive the best care for her specific needs and circumstances. On the other hand, if the nurse child steps in, the situation would likely be reversed. If the children acknowledge that the void left by Mama's stroke does not need to be filled by only one person, they might conclude that the wealth manager is now the best person to take care of Mama's assets while the nurse is the best person to take care of Mama herself. The obvious choice is for the wealth manager to manage the assets while the nurse attends to Mama's personal care. Mama will get the best care, and Mama's assets will get the best management if the two children do what they are good at and let the other sibling focus on the other thing. Thus, they should split the duties between themselves, rather than allow one of them to do all the work.

Economists refer to this as the "Guns and Butter." If Country A is very good at making guns, but poor at making butter, while Country B is poor at making guns, but very good at making butter, they will both be better off if each allocates its resources to the thing it is good at and trades its product for the product of the other country. Similarly, if a lord were building a castle, he would employ expert tradesmen for each particular task. He would bring in masons to lay stones and carpenters to cut wood. The lord would not use a jack of all trades to do both jobs.

The same applies in the example above. Mama will get the best care, and Mama's assets will get the best management if each child focuses on their own specific talent while trusting their sibling to do deploy their own skill towards Mama's care. A Sheriff typically will not do this. A Sheriff will strongarm his way into the Family Power Vacuum and try to do everything for Mama. Watch out for this.

The second thing family members will likely discover if they come together as a group to Build a Castle is that they will significantly reduce anxiety and resentment by filling the Family Power Vacuum slowly and methodically, according to an agreed plan in which all relevant family members have a say. In the example above, the wealth manager child might simply take over Mama's assets and direct the nurse child to provide Mama's physical care. That would not be Building a Castle. That would be the wealth manager filling the void unilaterally, and then delegating Mama's care to the other sibling. In contrast, if the children take the time to work together on a solution, come up with a plan, and implement that plan slowly as a group, then they will let the air back into the Vacuum slowly and minimize harm to the family.

Don't be discouraged if the Patriarch is the one who is most resistant to Building a Castle. Letting the air in slowly is about deploying the techniques in this book without the Patriarch's input or direction. A family can still Build a Castle even after the Patriarch cannot participate materially.

1.3.3   Enjoy the Fruits.

The next ancillary benefit to Building your Castle is that a Patriarch gets to enjoy the fruits of his labor. This benefit is life-enriching, and the key to understanding it is realizing that wealth is a tool rather than an end itself. Correlating personal success with the objective metrics of wealth is easy but wealth itself doesn't provide any direct benefit. You can't eat your money or take it with you when you die.

However, even modest wealth can be leveraged in ways that bring great joy and satisfaction. A Patriarch can leverage wealth to benefit the entire family and increase the likelihood that the family will enjoy long-term success. Done properly, this leads to greater satisfaction and contentment in life. The trick is to leverage wealth in ways that are productive and fair to the whole family.

To enjoy the fruits of his labor, a Patriarch will sometimes part with control of certain assets in exchange for something greater than what was given up. If possible, this should benefit everyone in the family in some special way. Sometimes, parting with control of assets also involves parting with possession of them or the ability to benefit from them at some future time. This is the case in the example of a family trip.

If the Patriarch has the means, why not bring the family on a trip to relax, reconnect, and bond? Most of us do this with our children when they're young but we may stop when the children become adults. This can be a prime opportunity to increase familial cohesion, establish traditions, share love, and bond. These are all major objectives for families that Build their Castles. And if future generations can join in, all the better.

By funding a family trip, a Patriarch necessarily parts with control, possession, and future benefit of certain assets, but there are ways to leverage this gambit and get more bang for your buck. For example, a family member can be tasked with planning the trip. This actually satisfies a number of Castle-Building goals: It enfranchises the organizer, decreases other family members' perceptions of monocratic control, allows the Patriarch to evaluate the family member's decision-making capabilities, frees up time for the Patriarch to focus on other things, builds confidence in both the Patriarch and the planner, and increases familial communication, just to name a few. The only cost associated with leveraging a trip in this way is giving up control.

Another possible way to leverage a family trip is to connect it with one or more personal interests, goals, or life events of one or more family members. For example, if a young family member is studying abroad in another country, the Patriarch might take the family to that country for a visit. This builds bonds between the family members because they get to witness a little piece of what will surely be a pivotal time in the student's life. This decision also demonstrates to the young family member that he or she is loved and that the Patriarch is interested in the young family member's choices.

1.3.4 Watch and Learn; Guide and Grow.

A primary concern for most Patriarchs is their children and other family members' ability to take control of the family assets. This concern is particularly acute where the family's primary asset is a closely held business. Studies have shown that most Patriarchs in this situation will bury their heads in the sand and ignore the issue. Rather than addressing the challenges of wealth transfer head-on, they ignore small problems until they grow into big problems and the family's choices are limited.

For example, most Patriarchs may feel that their children are unable to take over the family business even after the children reach adulthood. Eventually, the Patriarch will become disabled or die. Someone has to take over the business, but nobody is prepared to jump in full hog. The children may not understand how the business operates. They may lack the requisite business connections. They might have other careers or live in other parts of the country. In other words, instead of facing their children's lack of experience and know-how early on, most Patriarchs will put off teaching children about the family business.

Sadly, stories like this abound. They boil down to one common pattern: The Patriarch never thinks the children are ready to get involved. This notion starts when the children are young. Probably, the Patriarch is waiting for them to grow and mature just a little bit more in each successive year. But instead of helping the children out by creating some sort of introduction at a young age from where the children can expand their capabilities, the Patriarch continues to wait...until it's too late.

In contrast, Castle-Building Patriarchs enjoy seeing how family members react to and approach increased control of a family business. Patriarchs who embrace this transition are able to do two things: First, they assess each individual's maturity, competency, and growth over time. They quickly see who rises to the challenge of increased involvement. Second, they address and correct missteps at a more appropriate time and on a more appropriate level. This sort of guidance may prove crucial to the long-term survival of the business and ensure that the Patriarch leaves a truly impactful legacy.

Many Patriarchs find that the experience of watching their family members transition into positions of control over family businesses and other assets is in itself an ancillary benefit of Castle Building. This is no different than enjoying the fruits of one's labor. The pride and fulfillment that comes with a successful transition is almost unparalleled.

Of course, not everyone is well-suited to take over his Patriarch's business or other assets. That's fine. Where this is the case, it's far better for everyone involved if the Patriarch and family members reach this realization while the Patriarch is still alive and competent. This allows the Patriarch to assess other options. He or she may sell the business or transition existing employees into control positions. Neither of these options is nearly as bad as leaving loved ones to pick up the pieces of a business that has been broken by the Patriarch's disability or death.

Note as well that the benefits of watching children grow into the family business apply just as much in the context of managing family assets. Investing is a skill just like any other and for these purposes, it can be treated just like a business.

THE TOOLBOX

2.1 Generally.

Building a castle requires a lot of tools. No person or group of people could possibly do it with their bare hands. Trenches must be dug with shovels. Beams must be cut with saws, then joined by nails struck home with hammers. Stones must be lifted and set with cranes. The list goes on. The same principle applies with a family's Castle. A Patriarch who refuses to deploy and take advantage of the tools available will only build a house of cards. When the Family Power Vacuum whips through the kingdom, that house is sure to fall.

To suit each family's specific needs and unique situation, practitioners in various fields have developed an array of tools that can be deployed on an as-needed basis. Many are appropriate only for a very limited range of situations, and some are appropriate to most circumstances. Every Castle is different. It all depends on the particular family's needs at a given time.

This chapter provides an overview of the tools available so each family can deploy them as appropriate. Even if a given tool is not appropriate to your particular situation, knowing just a little bit about it may be helpful. Also, many of the tools below are themselves dynamic and may be shaped to fit a particular scenario.

2.2 Professionals.

Although it may not be entirely appropriate to think of people as tools, the broad array of professional services available to families can be daunting. Modern thinking supports the notion that a collaborative effort among professionals is the best avenue to success. When professionals from various disciplines work together, they can often avoid problems and mistakes that any one of them might make when working alone, absent the wisdom and cooperation of the others. On the other hand, getting a bunch of suits together in a room is an expensive way to spend one's day. As long as each member of a professional team is focused on clear goals, understands their particular role, and is willing to stick to their assigned role, this approach is definitely the best. But it is the Patriarch's responsibility to make sure things like petty rivalries and hairsplitting don't get in the way of progress.

Picking a professional who is right for a given family from among the many available is a major challenge, especially over the long term. For example, a well-kept secret in the legal community is that the basic level of proficiency required for a highly successful and lucrative legal career is, as it happens, quite low. To make things more confusing, there is an array of high-profile awards that are given to utterly undeserving professionals. Sometimes these awards are given out because the recipients provided some consideration to the awarding organization. Other times, the recipients have convinced other professionals (often in other fields) that they are the best in a given area. For example, an insurance broker might nominate a financial planner for an award thinking he is highly skilled, even though the insurance broker lacks the experience or technical know-how to appropriately evaluate him.

How can you find the professional that is right for you? For starters, you can look at a candidate's credentials. Specifically, what has the person actually earned? Board certification is generally a very good credential because it is very difficult to obtain. On the other hand, many deserving professionals cannot obtain board certification because their practice is too narrow to allow them to even sit for the exam. Also, there is an array of professional credentials nowadays that actually mean very little, so you may have to do a little research. Some professionals have gained valuable experience in previous careers, as might be the case with an accountant turned tax lawyer.

Although it flies in the face of our modern, digitally separated lifestyle, recommendations based on personal experiences are generally the best method of vetting professionals. If your friend or colleague had a good experience with a certain professional, you're likely to have a good experience too.

Finally, don't underestimate the value of a good personality match. The professional you pick should be someone you get along with. If you're comfortable speaking with your professional about deeply personal matters and able to communicate your thoughts effectively, you are much more likely to get a positive result.

Here are just a few of the professionals that might play a role in Building your Castle:

2.2.1 Attorneys.

Many Patriarchs employ an array of attorneys. These include estate planners, family lawyers, tax attorneys, litigators, securities lawyers, and real estate attorneys, as well as specialists in certain asset classes, such as aircraft.

One common misconception is that a few years in law school prepares a person to be proficient in all of these areas. Far from it. Effectively deploying the tools described in this chapter requires sophisticated training and years of experience. You wouldn't trust a stone mason's apprentice to build the castle tower, and you shouldn't trust an inexperienced attorney to address your family's legal needs without proper supervision.

When choosing an attorney, understanding the role that the attorney fills and what he or she brings to the table is helpful. The attorney is a technical master. He or she has significant training and, hopefully, experience which can be brought to bear on your particular situation. A transactional attorney is in the business of keeping you out of legal trouble you never knew existed. A litigation attorney is responsible for getting you out of trouble after a problem has occurred. Building your Castle is about employing the former so that you minimize your need of the latter.

But attorneys have their limitations too. They are not known for being a particularly creative bunch. They tend to view the world narrowly through the lens of their training which affirmatively disincentivizes them from thinking about unorthodox solutions to problems. They also want to avoid being blamed for giving bad advice, so they may shy away from areas which are more personal in nature. To put this another way, a family can spend great sums on the finest estate planning but still fall victim to the Family Power Vacuum when the Patriarch dies. To successfully Build your Castle, you will need more than the bare legal bones of the estate plan. Your family will need a succession plan and, although they may not be quick to admit it, this is beyond the scope of most estate planners' job description.

2.2.2 Investment Managers and Insurance Brokers.

Investment managers and insurance brokers often play a significant role in the Castle-Building team. Good investment managers will help clients look through the noise of modern markets. They will understand the ramifications of their clients' actions and keep an eye on market conditions. Good insurance brokers understand how to tailor policies for a given scenario and suggest the right solution for a given problem. Both investment managers and insurance brokers need to understand the tax and legal ramifications of their client's situation. An understanding of trusts is helpful too.

Bad investment managers and insurance brokers can be easy to spot. And there are a lot of them. Generally, the business models for these two areas are built on sales, so at least early on, these people will be rewarded most for signing up new clients. Fortunately, these peoples' lack of experience is mirrored by their lack of substantive knowledge because, despite what they tell you, they're not well trained. You can usually sniff them out with a few well-placed questions. If you don't know what to ask, your other professionals will. In fact, they will probably have a few people they can recommend who have shown the requisite mastery in their field.

2.2.3 Care Managers.

Care managers are invaluable to families caring for incapacitated loved ones. Although they typically assist with the care of elderly family members, care managers may prove useful in other circumstances as well. For example, they may be able to help with younger individuals who are incapacitated in much the same way as they assist with elderly clients. Care managers can also help improve relationships within a family. If, for example, Sister is caring for Mama in her old age, she might have a hard time explaining to Brother why her job is so difficult or expensive. Because she deals with geriatric clients on a regular basis, the family's care manager will both carry more authority with

Brother and be able to speak more concisely than Sister about what Mama really needs. Obviously, it's not a care manager's job to get between pugnacious or quarrelsome siblings, but they can sometimes stop an argument from starting in the first place, and that benefits the person under care significantly.

The role of a care manager is unique to the given situation, but his or her work generally relates to the management of a client's physical and psychological wellbeing. Most care managers have a nursing background and most will provide an array of services on an a-la-carte basis. They can coordinate between a client's doctors, manage medicines, and help keep eldercare facilities in line. Care managers generally do not provide business or asset management services. Trustees, attorneys-in-fact, asset managers, and guardians of a person's estate do that. But care managers will pay bills, manage household accounts, and the like.

Care managers can also guide family members as they navigate the daunting maze of medical and other issues that present themselves when a family member becomes disabled. This help includes not only advising on treatment decisions, but also assisting with administrative tasks, dealing with insurance, and informing the family about benefits and programs. Simply having a person around to sit in on quarterly care conferences at an elder care facility is well-worth the hourly fees most care managers charge. Care managers can quickly evaluate a client's medical record and suggest adjustments to medications and other treatments. They can advise on regulatory and compliance issues that inevitably crop up at care facilities. They will also ask questions the families don't know to ask. Families should always consider engaging a care manager to assist with the care of disabled family members.

2.2.4 CPAs.

Most families of means recognize the value of a quality accountant. Many studies have shown that accountants offer the best return on investment in the form of tax savings relative to the cost of services offered as compared with tax filing software or strip mall filing agencies.

On the other hand, many people fail to capitalize on their CPA's ability to provide transactional advice. CPAs can often provide valuable guidance when contemplating a given transaction.

What can be confusing, however, is where to draw the line between a CPA and a tax attorney. There is no hard and fast answer to this question and, in fact, many tax attorneys are former CPAs. Generally, however, the tax attorney acts as the strategic planner while the CPA focuses on a more tactical level. Also, attorneys, and not CPAs, should be the ones drafting documents, forming business entities, and the like. Some CPAs do these things without realizing that they are engaging in the unauthorized practice of law. But there is definitely overlap, so it will often behoove a family to consult both its CPA and its tax attorney before entering into a large transaction so that they can work together to accomplish the family's goals.

2.2.5 Genealogists.

Establishing a family narrative is a very important part of Building your Castle. A family narrative involves many inputs, but researching the family's ancestry and places of origin are an important piece. Although there are many self-help tools available to families, professionals will often uncover details that may not be found otherwise.

Genealogists are interesting. If a Patriarch is having trouble convincing his family to attend and participate in a Family Assembly or other Castle-Building strategies, inviting a genealogist might be a good way to incentivize participation. On the other hand, if a family is struggling to enfranchise a particular family member, appointing that person as the family genealogist may encourage participation from both the particular family member (who now has an opportunity to shine) as well as other family members (who will be interested in what the family member has to report).

2.2.6 Appraisers.

Appraisers play a vital role in effective Castle building because they act as equalizers. Family businesses and other assets (such as real estate) are notoriously difficult to value. Most estate plans (and intestacy laws) punt on the issue of dividing assets by calling for *prorata* division of everything in an estate. That is, standard operating procedure typically requires each heir to receive a proportionate share of each individual asset. But this is often inappropriate for a given family.

Consider this hypothetical scenario: Martha mom, the widowed Matriarch (who never remarried), has three surviving children (all also the children of David dad, the deceased Patriarch), Adam, Betsy, and Connor, and no predeceased children. Let's also say that Martha has three primary assets: a house, where she and Adam live, a business started by David but currently managed by Betsy, and a brokerage account. Connor lives in another city and has his own career. Does it make sense for Adam, Betsy, and Connor to get each get 1/3 of the house, the business, and the brokerage account? Of course not. Wouldn't it make more sense for Adam to get the house, Betsy to get the business, and Connor to get the brokerage account? Maybe. It all depends on the relative value of the assets. That's where appraisers come in. They can help equalize the disposition of Martha's assets fairly (according to value) among the children and thereby enable their proper distribution (according to personal circumstances).

Keep in mind that this equalizing function is not limited to considerations at the time of (or while planning for) Martha's death. The same principles apply when a Patriarch makes significant gifts to family members and is also important in the context of contingency planning and control transition between various family members.

Appraisers can also function to ease tensions significantly among family members. Effective communication among family members is a big part of Building your Castle. You can't communicate effectively unless you have accurate information at hand. By obtaining proper and professional guidance as to the value of your assets, you will be better equipped to discuss them with your family.

2.2.7 Facilitators.

In this Book, a "**Facilitator**" is a person who manages and directs your Family Assembly (see Section 2.3 below). This person will interview family members before the Assembly, develop an agenda, and conduct the actual meeting. As an independent third party, a Facilitator can greatly enhance the experience of an Assembly. He or she can set expectations, provide time management, hold accountability, and manage personalities. He or she can also bring professional experience to bear on your family's particular situation and help you develop solutions to issues that you may not have thought of yourself.

Good Facilitators have a unique mix of characteristics that make them successful. They have to be technically proficient in things like estate planning, personal finance, real estate transactions, tax, fiduciary duties, medical care, insurance, and government benefits, just to name a few. On the other hand, they also need to be personable. They should be diplomatic and approachable. They should not be intimidating, stuffy, or boring. A good Facilitator should also be accepting and nonjudgmental. At the end of the day, a good Facilitator will help the work of Building your Castle seem more like fun and games than necessary drudgery.

Facilitators may have been attorneys, financial advisors, or even family counselors in a previous career.

Indeed, they may continue those other activities in concert with facilitation work. In order to eliminate bias, most families prefer to use an independent third party as their Facilitator. For example, the family attorney may be too closely involved with certain family members to make all family members feel comfortable. On the other hand, many large banks will offer facilitators as part of their private client services. In that case, even though the Facilitator works for an institution the family uses, the Facilitator is sufficiently removed from the family's business to be effective. Families that don't have enough assets to qualify for private client services will have to seek out their own Facilitator and pay a fee for their service.

2.2.8 Trustees.

Trustees are the people who manage trusts. They owe a fiduciary duty to the beneficiaries of the trusts they manage. A trustee's responsibility is to carry out the intent of the trust for the beneficiary's benefit. Trustees can be corporations—many banks have trust departments—or they can be individuals. A trust beneficiary can even serve as its trustee in most circumstances.

There is a reason why they call trusts trusts. When selecting a trustee, picking a person who has the wherewithal to understand his or her duties and the good moral character to fulfill those duties properly is crucial. Many people select corporate trustees because their trust departments are staffed by professionals who understand what the job calls for and are well-suited to perform their duties without making mistakes. And if they do make a mistake, corporate trustees generally have deep pockets, so any damages can generally be recovered from them.

On the other hand, corporate trustees often charge very high fees which eat away at trust assets. Most, if not all, states allow corporate trustees to charge trustees' fees and also collect fees for investment management or banking services. Thus, corporate trustees are disincentivized from making trust distributions because they effectively get to double dip on fees. Corporate trustees also tend to be more cautious about trust distributions. If a beneficiary wants money from his or her trust, corporate trustees will often require a formal, written request explaining the reason for the distribution. The request will then be discussed by a committee, which must approve the distribution before it can be made. Not only is this invasive, it's also time-consuming.

Conversely, individual trustees, particularly family members, tend to have a more intimate knowledge of the family. These personal relationships facilitate proper management and distribution of trust assets. Related parties also tend to charge much less, if anything, in fees. On the other hand, individual trustees, by definition, are only human. Trustee duties are extremely complicated and confusing. If an individual makes a mistake while acting as trustee, there will often be no way for a beneficiary to recover because the trustee will not have sufficient assets to make the beneficiary whole.

To resolve some of the problems described above, lawyers are becoming creative in their drafting. For example, it is increasingly popular to either divide trustees' duties such that a Corporate Trustee will conduct much of the day-to-day bookkeeping and investment management duties while an individual will make major decisions regarding investments and distributions. This arrangement is generally called a "directed trust." Alternatively, a trustee might be subject to oversight by one or more people with special powers. A single person with this power is typically called a "trust protector," and a group of such people may be referred to as a "trust committee," "trust council," or some other term. Depending on how the trust is set up, a Trust Protector may have the power to carry out (or prevent) certain actions and/or make the Trustee carry them out (or prevent them).

2.3 Family Assembly.

The cornerstone of most Castle-Building endeavors is a "**Family Assembly**." These are so important that an entire chapter in this book is dedicated to them. Put simply, the Family Assembly is the time when families get together to discuss and plan family business. Family Assemblies are often held in conjunction with a family trip or significant decision that impacts family members. Many families hold their assemblies annually, but some meet more often.

Family Assemblies are often run by Facilitators. Family Assemblies should be upbeat and fun, but they should also be professional. A major challenge for the Facilitator is balancing the mundane and often tedious work at an Assembly with the fun parts that get everyone excited to be there.

Family Assemblies vary widely in duration, scope, tone, frequency, and many other factors. Some go on for weeks, while others are held in a single day. It all depends on the nature of the family and their business. For a family of moderate wealth that meets annually, however, a Family Assembly often takes place over two or three days.

2.4   Family Mission Statement.

Developing a "**Family Mission Statement**" in the Castle-Building context has two major benefits. The first, more obvious, benefit is that the Family Mission Statement provides guidance for the family. When any family member reaches a time of indecision, he or she may look to the Family Mission Statement for guidance. The Family Mission Statement might also be called upon when considering any number of other decisions as a family. Where will we live? Where will we go on vacation? What schools will the kids attend? What charities will the family support? All of these decisions can be easier with a Family Mission Statement.

The second benefit of a Family Mission Statement is less obvious. By going through the process of coming up with the statement itself, a family has to go through some introspection and soul-searching. The family benefits from this process because it provides clarity and focus.

There is no right or wrong way to create a Family Mission Statement, but the process may go a little like this: Hold a Family Assembly. The Facilitator, the Patriarch, or another family member who is chosen to be moderator might start the process with a few questions to get the ball rolling. These questions should generally focus on the family's values, ideals and priorities. The goal is to brainstorm ideas in a healthy discussion. Once the process starts, anyone can ask questions as long as he doesn't hijack the conversation. The moderator's job is to prevent this from happening without putting anyone out or appearing to play favorites. As the questions come out, the moderator can write down the answers, taking down as much as possible and editing or cutting the Mission Statement down later.

Here are some example questions:

- How does the family feel about marriage and what is its purpose?
- How do we want to treat each other?
- How do we want to treat others?
- How do we want others to see us?
- How do we want to handle finances?
- What principles are important to our family?
- What roles will each of us have?
- Where do we, as a family, come from?
- What traditions do we bring with us from the families in which we were raised?
- What do we do for fun?
- What traditions do want to create and keep?
- How do we want to give back?
- What do we find embarrassing or distasteful?
- What are we good at individually? As a family?
- Who do we look up to and why?
- Where do we find inspiration?
- How do we feel about art and culture?
- How do we feel about service to our country?
- What makes us unique?

- What do we excel at *and* what needs improvement?

This brainstorming process is about getting ideas out there. No answer is wrong or unimportant. If it comes to anyone's mind, it's worth consideration, even if that consideration ultimately results in rejection. The simple act of rejecting ideas might be just as important as accepting others because this might remove the mental clutter that can lead to indecision down the road.

As the family brainstorms, be on the lookout for themes. You may even take a breakout session to let individuals or small groups organize the answers into thematic groups. Once the themes are recognized, the family can begin the process of boiling them down to those which are most important and arranging them into concise and powerful statements. Creativity comes into play here and a good measure of hair-splitting is standard, so it is important to be patient. After all, this process is supposed to be fun!

Once the family has settled on the wording of the mission statement, it is important to write it down and distribute it to the entire family. The Family Mission Statement needs to be repeated regularly to remind each family member of his or her direction and the lessons learned while it was being developed.

Finally, here are a few tips that might be helpful in thinking about and creating a Family Mission Statement:

- There is no right or wrong answer.
- There is no right or wrong way to create a Family Mission Statement, but results will almost always be better where each family member

feels fully enfranchised and respected.
- The Family Mission Statement can be changed over time.
- The Family Mission Statement can be any length, but most families will want to keep it short.
- Listen to other family member's ideas and be respectful.
- The more they're involved, the more likely your family members will live in the spirit of the Family Mission Statement.
- Don't bring up the Family Mission Statement unexpectedly.

2.5 Family Constitution.

Organization is the key to any system, and a "**Family Constitution**" sets out the procedures that enable the family to function in an organized, orderly fashion with minimal conflict. The Family Constitution is basically the set of bylaws under which the family operates. It sets out policies and procedures for the family to follow as well as the rights and responsibilities of each family member. This not only provides structure, which is beneficial on a practical level, but it also promotes predictability, which reduces fear and anxiety. Since it's human nature to act irrationally when we're afraid or anxious, a reduction in fear and anxiety means increased rational behavior among family members and better decision-making.

People sometimes wonder how a Family Constitution differs from a Family Mission Statement. A Family Mission Statement answers the *what* whereas a Family Constitution answers the *how*. That is, the Family Mission Statement is an expression of what a family is all about whereas the Family Constitution let's everyone know how they're going to get there. You can also think of a Family Mission Statement as a strategic plan while a Family Constitution provides the tactical procedures for the family's regular and orderly operation. Family Mission Statements are also much shorter than Family Constitutions. A typical Family Mission Statement is, at most a few sentences long, whereas a Family Constitution will often go on for pages. Finally, Family Constitutions are not appropriate for every family. They can be overwhelming, stuffy, or too restrictive, particularly with smaller families. Larger families benefit much more from Family Constitutions. On the other hand, nearly every family will benefit from a Family Mission Statement.

Without question, a Family Constitution is one of the more formal tools for Building your Castle. Not only must the family go to the trouble of conceiving and drafting it, but they must follow it as well. This requires a concerted effort over years.

Here are some topics that might be addressed in a Family Constitution:

2.5.1 Decision-making.

Who will be the decision-makers for the family and what decisions can they make? When must the entire family (or some other group) be consulted? How many votes, if any, will the various people have? Do all family members at every generational level get the same vote? Will decision-making be centralized in a board or advisory committee or decentralized among various family members?

2.5.2 Identification.

Who are the family members? What does it take to be a family member and what will get you expelled from the family? How are various family members classified, and what are the rights and responsibilities of the various classes?

2.5.3 Enfranchisement.

How and when will younger generations be indoctrinated in the family business and/or made aware of family assets? When will they be allowed to join the family business or participate in decision-making? Should spouses of family members be allowed or encouraged to participate, and if so, to what extent? What should be done with family members who do not wish to participate?

2.5.4 Dispute resolution.

Will disputes be arbitrated internally, and if so, by whom? How will dispute resolution become binding? Will internal arbitrators be compensated for their time, and if so, by whom?

2.5.5 Stewardship.

Who will manage the family business and/or other assets? Will it be a group or an individual? Should certain decisions be made only with the consent of additional family members? Will any constraints be placed on the managing individual or body?

2.5.6 Appointments.

What roles can the various family members fill and how long should they fill them? Examples include:

- Historian
- News Letter Editor
- Investment Manager
- Caregiver/Responsible Person
- Secretary/Communications Director
- Project Manager
- Meeting Planner/Organizer
- Arbitrator
- Vacation Property Manager
- Art & Collectibles Curator

2.5.7 Meetings.

How and when will the family meet to discuss family business on a regular basis? What procedures are needed to call a meeting in an emergency? Must meetings be held in person, or may they be held electronically?

2.5.8 Amendments.

How and when can the Family Constitution be amended? How is an incapacitated family member represented in the amendment process?

2.5.9 Consequences.

What happens when someone doesn't follow the terms of the Family Constitution? Who will enforce the rules? What must be done before enforcement can take place? Will the Patriarch be subject to enforcement and if so, to what extent?

2.5.10 Emergency Procedures.

What will happen in a natural disaster or emergency? What will happen when a family member, especially the Patriarch, becomes incapacitated?

2.5.11 Divorce.

What happens when family members divorce? Can divorced parties still function effectively as family members? Must a divorcing spouse be bought out of the family business, and if so, on what terms?

2.5.12 Respect.

What standards of respect are required of family members? How are family members expected to treat each other on birthdays, holidays, and anniversaries, or upon the death of a family member? What traditions do the family members acknowledge and agree to follow?

2.5.13 Religion/Morals/Values.

Is there a common view in the family on religion and if so, can it be clearly stated? Does the family hold any morals or values in such high esteem that it wants to mention them in the constitution? How can these views be changed over time? What happens if a minority of family members does not agree with the rest?

2.5.14 Care for Elderly.

Who will be responsible for caring for elderly family members? What procedures should a family have in place for determining when a family member is incapacitated or unable to conduct certain tasks, such as drive a car?

2.5.15 Exclusivity.

Is being a member of the family exclusive or can a person properly hold allegiance to more than one family?

2.5.16 Departure.

How does an individual or subgroup leave the family of their own accord? Must they be bought out of the family business?

2.5.17 Holidays.

How will issues surrounding holidays be handled? Which holidays call for a gathering of most or all of the family, and who will host those gatherings?

As should be fairly obvious at this point, a Family Constitution can get pretty bulky. As a general rule, Family Constitutions are most useful in the context of a large or extended family. But that doesn't mean small families can't benefit from a Family Constitution as well. Like all of the other tools described in this chapter, each family is free to pick and choose as much or as little as is right for it. Some Family Constitutions are very short indeed.

An alternative to a lengthy and detailed Family Constitution is for a family to agree on a relatively generalized Family

Constitution, and then set out the more specific policies and procedure for the family in a policy manual or similar document. This structure can function especially well where decision-making authority is concentrated in a small group of people relative to the entire family. Under this model, the decision-maker(s) are granted authority, generally within certain limits, to lay out or alter the policies and procedures without the need for a full-family vote. This can make for more convenient administration of the family's business. On the other hand, it also removes control from certain family members and vests it in an individual or small group.

Another alternative is to create a constitution that mostly binds the Patriarch. This model can be effective where a Patriarch wishes to maintain primary control over most family functions while also providing some guarantees to other family members. It is somewhat like a constitutional monarchy.

2.6 Family History Narrative.

The **"Family History Narrative"** is one of the most fun tools in the toolbox. It may be oral, written, or preserved in any number of mediums. In essence, the Family History Narrative is just what it sounds like: It is the story of the family. It is important because it fosters unity and a sense of belonging. Generally, a Family History Narrative is recited or discussed at the beginning of each Family Assembly, and it is intended to get the family members excited about their family unit.

A Family History Narrative builds comradery and boosts morale among family members because it creates a sense of identity and belonging. It also highlights a shared struggle that the family can be a part of, even if the real struggle happened in previous generations. In the US, we do something similar every Fourth of July when we go to watch fireworks or shoot off our own. None of us survived the Revolutionary War, but blowing stuff up sure does make us all feel more American, right? Psychologically, this tradition allows us to live vicariously through our predecessors and come together as a group. A Family History Narrative should do the same thing for your family. If your family's Castle has already been built, tell the story of how it was built in a way that allows the current family members to feel the struggle themselves. If you are in the process of Building your Castle, tell this in a way that will sharpen individual family members' resolve to keep working towards the common goal.

A Family History Narrative can be as detailed or general as the family likes. It may answer questions such as:

- What country is the family from?
- When and how did the family come to America?
- How was the family wealth accumulated, and what did it take to accumulate that wealth?
- What are the family's most important traditions?
- Does the family use any special mannerisms, gestures, or phrases?
- What foods are important to the family?
- What values did the family leverage to gain its wealth?

2.7 Family Counsel.

A Family Counsel can mean different things in different situations. It may serve as the family's decisions-making body, much like a board of directors does for a company. Alternatively, it may function as a tribunal for dispute resolution. It may even be both.

Family Counsels generally serve large families where the wealth and power have already been disbursed. In smaller families, the Family Counsel is often a counsel of one (or two), namely the Patriarch (and possibly the Patriarch's spouse).

The way in which a Family Counsel functions is generally laid out in a Family Constitution.

2.8 Committees.

Many families may benefit from the formation of one or more committees which take on various tasks and business of the family. Examples might include:

- Grievance Committee
- Investment Management Committee
- Spouse's Committee
- Education, Training, and Enrichment Committee
- Family Assistance Committee
- Social Committee
- Art and Collectibles Committee
- Family History Committee
- Philanthropy Committee

- Fiduciary Committee
- Ranch Committee
- Caregiver Committee
- Holiday Committee.

Provisions for the committees can be set out in a Family Constitution and a Facilitator can help craft the language under which each committee will operate.

2.9 Comprehensive Estate Plan.

Estate planning is a cornerstone of Building your Castle. A **"Comprehensive Estate Plan"** is more than just a Will or a trust. It is a thoughtful, well-crafted, and properly documented plan that is designed to minimize **"Coverage Gaps"** and **"Logic Bombs."** Coverage Gaps are periods where management and control get lost for one reason or another. For example, if a person does not have a durable power of attorney, a Coverage Gap exists for the period when he is alive but incapacitated: When the person is not incapacitated, he manages and controls his own assets. When the person dies, management and control of his assets are provided by an executor under their Will. But when the person becomes incapacitated, no other person can step in and provide the needed management and control without opening a formal guardianship through a court. Nobody wants that.

Logic Bombs, on the other hand, occur when things do not go according to plan. The particular wording of legal documents sometimes causes an unwanted result. For example, let's say Paul Patriarch's Will provides that, upon his death, Paul's estate is to be split between his three children, April, Bill, and Charlie. But Bill dies before Paul, leaving a son (Paul's grandson), Gregg. In such a case, Paul probably wants Bill's share of the inheritance to pass down to Gregg. Most people expect this will happen and it might, but it also might not. Depending on the wording of Paul's Will, as well as applicable state law, Bill's share might get divided between April and Charlie, to the exclusion of Gregg. This example is a Logic Bomb. Estate planners have to take much care to avoid situations like this.

A Comprehensive Estate Plan typically includes most or all of the following documents:

- Last Will and Testament (may be a "Pourover Will" if the primary dispositive mechanism is a revocable living trust)
- Revocable Living Trust (maybe, depending on the circumstances)
- Durable Power of Attorney (for financial matters)
- Directive to Physicians (for end-of-life decisions)
- Medical Power of Attorney (for non-end-of-life decisions)
- HIPAA release (may be included in medical power of attorney)
- Declaration of guardian (in the event of incapacity)
- Declaration of guardian for minor children
- Appointment of Agent for Disposition of Remains (so your family doesn't fight over your remains)
- Statement of Anatomical Gift (for those who want to give their body to medical science)

While a deep dive into the Comprehensive Estate Plan is beyond the scope of this book, understanding how estate planning fits within the analogy of the family's Castle is important. If we stretch the analogy a little more, it will make more sense: As a matter of simple geometry, the floor plan of a real castle must have at least three corners. It probably has a lot more than three, but three is the minimum because otherwise, it can't be an enclosed shape. Thus, if the estate plan is a cornerstone of your family Castle, there must also be at least two other cornerstones for it to stand. That is, your family Castle must have at least two other major components that are just as critical as its estate plan.

In practice, this concept is easy to prove. There are lots and lots of families that don't survive the Family Power Vacuum despite their very high-quality (and often very expensive) estate planning. It happens all the time. What this means is that estate planning alone won't get you there. You need the Comprehensive Estate Plan, for sure, but if you're going to Build your Castle, you've got to do more. Every cornerstone has to be strong enough to hold up in the face of an attack.

Whereas it is a given that a Comprehensive Estate Plan is a cornerstone of every family Castle, the other cornerstones are not so readily apparent. Indeed, they change from family to family because every family's Castle is different. Each has its own unique footprint. Communication and expectation both come up regularly, although they are far less prevalent as cornerstones than estate planning. Families that communicate well and keep their expectations realistic when it comes to power and inheritance tend to get through tough times unscathed. Other cornerstones could also be religion or spirituality, education, and collective perseverance or struggle.

2.10 Trusts.

There are so many different trust options to choose from when Building your Castle that practitioners sometimes call them collectively an alphabet soup. They are known by abbreviations such as RLT, RMT, CRAT, CRUT, GRAT, SNT, GRUT, ILIT, IGIT, and so forth. All these different kinds of trusts address a wide array of issues a family might face. These include:

- Protecting assets from creditors and spouses
- Reducing income tax exposure
- Reducing Transfer Tax exposure
- Caring for elderly family members
- Caring for family members with special needs
- Protecting loved ones from their own weaknesses
- Increasing privacy and security
- Providing continuity of and/or centralized management of assets
- Accepting assets that certain people are forbidden by law from inheriting
- Leveraging charitable gifts
- Maximizing retirement plan benefits
- Avoiding probate
- Holding life insurance

The list goes on. The key is working closely with good attorneys and other professionals who can help you identify which of these tools should be deployed and then help you wield them properly for a stated goal.

2.11 Guardianship.

Often referred to as the "nuclear bomb" of options, guardianship is a place few of us ever want to go. Every guardianship is the relationship between two people, a guardian and a ward. In a guardianship, the guardian's job is to take care of the ward. The relationship is very similar to that of parent and child.

Guardianships break down into two major categories: guardianships of the person and guardianships of the estate. A guardian of the person is responsible for managing a ward's daily affairs. The guardian chooses where the ward will live, what the ward will do each day, and what clothes the ward will wear. A guardian of the estate is responsible for managing the ward's financial affairs.

There are two primary instances where guardianship comes up in the context of Building your Castle. If a family member has special needs, it may be appropriate to seek guardianship over him. In certain circumstances, Guardianship may be the best way to manage any public benefits a person is entitled to. Alternatively, it can also be necessary to seek guardianship over someone who, because of old age, an illness, or some accident, has become mentally incompetent and can no longer manage his affairs.

Most people generally try to avoid guardianship for a number of reasons. First, getting guardianship over someone necessarily means taking away their civil rights. By definition, a ward cannot make decisions for himself because a court has stepped in and taken that freedom away. Second, guardianships are very public and disruptive. The process of obtaining guardianship happens in open court and on the public record. Not only can this be embarrassing for the family, but it is also physically and emotionally taxing on all parties. Third, guardianship is very expensive. Even a "simple" guardianship will often set a family back tens of thousands of dollars in fees. A guardianship always involves at least two lawyers, then there are things like court costs, doctors' fees (to declare the ward incompetent), bonds, and much more. If a dispute over the guardianship arises, these costs can go up dramatically. On top of all that, the guardian will have to pay an attorney to make regular reports to the probate court for as long as the guardianship lasts. No wonder families go to such great lengths to avoid this mess!

What can be done to prevent (or at least mitigate) a guardianship? Well, for a competent adult who is worried about facing guardianship in the future, the best defense is a good Comprehensive Estate Plan. Guardianship can often be avoided with proper medical and financial powers of attorney in place. Trusts can also be very helpful. Of course, all of this must be set up while the person is still competent.

Where a person has always been incompetent, coordinated trust planning by other family members is generally the best option. Unlike the competent adult who is concerned with protecting assets after he or she loses competency, the family of the incompetent child is concerned about losing public benefits if he or she inherits any assets. By directing those assets to certain trusts, the ward can reap the benefit of those assets without losing the public benefits.

In either case, communication is the key to success. If a Patriarch is trying to avoid guardianship, he should set out his

Comprehensive Estate Plan and also communicate his wishes to family members so that they all understand their respective roles if and when the time comes. If a family is concerned about a family member with special needs, they should communicate with one another to be sure that any potential inheritance goes to the right trust.

2.12 Asset Protection Plans.

There are many books written about asset protection, so it is largely outside the purview of this book. But almost any family that is Building a Castle will need some sort of asset protection planning, so a few notes are appropriate here.

Asset protection planning can mean all sorts of different things, depending on the particular facts and circumstances. The end result usually depends on three questions: First, how likely is it that a plaintiff might bring a lawsuit against a member of the family? Second, what particular laws could a plaintiff bring to bear in a particular scenario? Third, how much expense and hassle will the family tolerate in defense of its assets?

The family's lawyers can advise on the specifics of your family's particular asset protection needs, but generally, business entities (corporations, LLCs, limited partnerships, etc.) and certain kinds of trusts are the legal mechanisms for providing the desired protection. Homestead protections and certain statutorily-protected assets also come into play. Although they have fallen out of favor since their heyday in the 1990s, international planning strategies can be used for asset protection as well.

Most families that are Building a Castle will have some asset protection strategies. A family business will typically be organized as an LLC, limited partnership, or corporation, and other assets will often be held in trust. Similarly, rental real estate will often be held in a business entity to protect the family.

The family's lawyers will advise on the appropriateness, extent, and form of asset protection planning in a given scenario. But that's not Building your Castle. Building your Castle means taking a step beyond the mere legal work of establishing a framework that provides the protection. To really Build your Castle, you also have to educate your family members about that framework and teach them how to manage it when you are gone. If the family doesn't understand the asset protection planning, it doesn't matter how good it is because the family can (and often will) squander it internally.

Assets that are squandered as a result of the Family Power Vacuum are just as lost to the family as assets that are taken by a creditor. Asset protection planning is designed to thwart external threats. It does not lessen internal threats. If anything, it increases those threats because it can be difficult to understand and it often obscures information (leading to fear, irrational behavior, etc.).

The castle, once again, makes a great analogy: Think of your asset protection planning as the physical structure of your Castle. It is the walls, the moat, and the timbers. You want these to be strong to protect against invaders. And there are many highly skilled, knowledgeable attorneys who will be happy to help you build them to withstand the strongest enemies. But if you don't teach your children how to conduct the daily maintenance on your Castle, the walls will crumble. If you don't teach them how to cook safely in the kitchen, they might burn the whole thing down. If you don't teach them how to man and use your Castle's defenses, it will be overrun. Building your Castle is all about avoiding exactly these problems.

Note as well that asset protection planning has a tendency to restrict access to cash. Uneducated members of wealthy families will expect to see cash when a Patriarch dies. When this cash fails to materialize quickly, those family members often start causing problems.

2.13 Life Insurance.

We tend to think of life insurance as a way to provide for our family when we're no longer able to do so ourselves: pay premiums now and maybe get proceeds later. Insurance can do this, but it can also be much more.

Life insurance companies are constantly developing new products to offer their customers to fill a variety of needs, both during life and after death. Life insurance can provide liquidity to pay estate tax and other expenses. It can be used to fund a buy-sell agreement, or offset disparities in a Comprehensive Estate Plan. Life insurance can also be used as an investment and a tool for protecting assets or providing credit.

The point is that there are many uses for life insurance beyond what we're used to. An experienced planner will be able to help you determine what kinds of coverage you might need and how to price them effectively. Of course, life insurance is not a cure-all, but it is something people should generally be open to.

2.14 Intra-Family Loans.

Loans between family members are a fantastic tool. They allow loved ones to access and leverage wealth without depleting it. They also teach financial responsibility and the value of a dollar, as well as the importance of good record-keeping.

Like any loan, an intra-family loan follows certain well-established tax rules. The loan itself is not taxable, nor is the return of principal. The interest that is charged, however, is taxable as ordinary income to the lender. If the borrower is a business (such as a child's controlled corporation), then the interest may be deductible by the business.

If you want to use loans to Build your Castle, two things are important. First, the loan has to be set up properly. It should be documented properly, in the form of a note (and possibly also a loan agreement). The note should also bear the proper amount of interest. If the interest is too low, a taxable gift can occur, and if it is too high, usury laws might apply. The rules surrounding these problems are very complex, so it is important to have the guidance of a good lawyer. Also, if a loan will be secured by collateral, a proper security agreement and filing under the Uniform Commercial Code, if applicable, are very important.

Second, the loan must be respected. This means that the loan is not a sham from the beginning. Disguising a gift so it looks like a loan to the IRS or creditors can get you into a lot of hot water. Generally, intra-family loans are subject to a heightened level of legal scrutiny, and a substance over form analysis will apply to determine what the transaction really is. During the term of the loan, it is also very important that payments are made on time, the right amount of interest is charged, good records are kept, and if necessary, collateral is foreclosed on.

In addition to the practical impact that intra-family loans can have—namely, providing the use of your assets without depleting your own net worth—they also have a significant psychological impact. Loans send very clear messages. Whoever receives the loan knows they're not getting a free lunch. To other family members, a loan signifies that you are not playing favorites.

One other important consideration needs to be thought through before an intra-family loan is made: What will happen if the family member fails to pay the loan back? Assume Dad loans Son $200,000 to start a business and it fails. Assuming the loan is properly made and documented, Dad has several options. He can do nothing and simply forgive the loan. He can sue Son. He can renegotiate the terms of the loan. He can even make offsetting gifts to other children.

Each of these options will have different ramifications. For example, doing nothing could lead the IRS to hold that the loan was a sham from the beginning, and forgiving the loan would likely cause Son to pick up additional taxable income to the extent of the amount forgiven. The best course of action depends on the facts and circumstances, but Dad should have a backup plan ready in case the loan agreement is not successfully repaid.

2.15 Gifts.

Gifts are similar to loans in two ways. First, both allow for someone other than the initial holder to benefit from the funds. Second, they are both subject to a plethora of tax and other legal rules. However, that is where the similarity stops.

Gifts are subject to one of the three transfer taxes, namely the federal gift tax. The rules surrounding gift tax are quite complex, but families with large estates often use these rules to their advantage to maximize the benefits they offer. Most of this planning centers around two rules. The first is the "annual exclusion," which allows people to make small gifts without incurring gift tax. Using this rule, families often enter into gifting programs that shift large sums to their children and further descendants over time. Families often make these gifts in trust, which requires additional planning. The second rule allows people to make unlimited gifts to pay for tuition or medical expenses. Using this rule, families can shift even more wealth. The catch with the medical and tuition exclusion is that gifts have to be made directly to the institutions charging the tuition or medical fees. If, for example, Grandfather gives $20,000 to Son to pay for Granddaughter's surgery, the exclusion does not apply. It makes no difference what Son actually does with the money. To get the exemption, Grandfather must pay the hospital, doctor, and other medical providers directly.

A few more gift tax rules are important. First, gift taxes apply to the gratuitous transfer of any property, which may or may not be cash. A transfer is gratuitous to the extent the value of whatever is given exceeds the fair market value of whatever, if anything, is received in return. Thus, Dad can't sell Daughter the ranch for $1. If the ranch is worth $1,000,000 when Dad does this, he will be deemed to have made a gift of $999,999. Second, gift tax is imposed on the giver, not the recipient. Finally, as with loans, a substance over form analysis will apply to gifts, so if the practical effect of some transfer is the same as a gift, it will be treated as a gift.

But gift tax should not be the only concern for those who go about Building their Castle. It's just as important that the Patriarch consider the broader impacts that gifts will have on the family.

Large gifts are the norm in some families, but not in others. It depends on the personalities involved. For families that do make gifts, however, all members of a given generational level need to understand the purpose and intended meaning behind the gifts. Gifting that is perceived as unequal by children or other family members can cause animosity. Where possible and practical, gifts should generally be equal at a given generational level.

Gifts should also be transparent. A Patriarch may attempt to give assets to a particular child in secret, but that secret is likely to get out. When it does, it will create animosity among the other children. Similarly, it may lead the benefitting child to feel entitled, which may worsen the problem. Far better for the Patriarch to make the gift in the open. That is, around the time of the gift, the Patriarch should inform the other children about the gift and explain why the one child received it. By doing this, the Patriarch can lessen the animosity and, correspondingly, irrational behavior of the children. Also, a Patriarch may come to the realization that his inequitable behavior is unwarranted and either lessen the amount of the gift, forgo it altogether, or make equal gifts to other family members.

RECOGNIZING AND LEVERAGING VAROIUS FAMILY PERSONALITIES

3.1   The Lord as Project Manager.

Let's think a little bit about how the feudal system was supposed to have worked in days of old. The reality may have been far from this ideal, but let's pretend that things went as advertised:

The lord of a castle was a manager of people. Construction of a castle involved an array of different journeymen and master craftsmen who specialized in all sorts of trades. Stonecutting, carpentry, and metal working were just a few of these. There were throngs of unskilled workers too. What's more, once the castle was built, a veritable army was needed to run it (not to mention the actual army it took to secure it). Cooks, washerwomen, pig boys, watchmen, and chambermaids all did their parts. Ultimately, the lord was responsible for keeping this community in order and guaranteeing their safety.

In addition to managing the household for his own comfort, the lord of the manner also had other concerns and responsibilities. The feudal system is well known for its serfs, who were obliged to work the land for their lord. Less well known, however, are the obligations that flowed in the opposite direction. For example, the lord was obliged to provide protection and housing for the serfs. The lord also had to provide justice (such as it was) and land which serfs could work for their own sustenance.

Ideally, the lord was responsible for the wellbeing, both physical and moral, of those who served him. This naturally motivated the lord to make the most efficient use of the various people around him. That is, if the lord were required to give someone shelter, he might as well make him useful in the fields, or if possible, encourage his training in a technical skill.

A lord had little choice in who would be at his disposal and under his protection. Today, anyone can find an employee by posting an ad online and sifting through a wide array of candidates vying for the position. The employer enjoys the luxury of being selective. In contrast, the lord of a castle had to make do with what he had, so if a person needed a job, something, no matter how trivial, was found. Not only would this maximize the lord's wealth, but it also kept the person busy, lest he plot some sort of rebellion.

On the other hand, the use of force was not a particularly effective tool for the lord, so he only used it as a last resort.

Until the development of modern firearms, the effective use of force was a matter of strength, both in terms of physicality and numbers. In contemporary times, arresting an unruly man requires little more than another person with a gun, but in the old days, it would have required a man or group of men who were stronger than the first. Since this was inefficient, skills of persuasion and leadership were much more valuable.

All of these principles apply to any Patriarch Building a Castle. Building a Castle requires a wide array of talents and skills, and it takes even more to maintain the Castle. Also, with only a few exceptions, we don't get to pick our family members. For the most part, we're stuck with the people we get. Finally, it is generally ineffective for a Patriarch to bend other family members to his will by force or manipulation. Other methods are far more efficient and will generally lead to much greater happiness overall. Indeed, we can't actually force our family members to do anything (at least not legally), but we can put them to hard decisions, and it can be tempting for a Patriarch to do this without concern for the perspective of the person being bent. The textbook example of this is when a Patriarch cuts off a dependent child for some miscreant behavior. Because of the tendency to engender animosity among various family members, tactics such as this should only be deployed when absolutely necessary. We will talk more about this in Chapter 5.

3.2 Acceptance as a First Step.

Curiosity may have killed the cat, but families die on unspoken dreams. Patriarchs often have tremendous difficulty accepting that their children and other family members aren't like them. Stated more broadly, it's frustrating that our kids don't respond predictably to certain stimuli. It's easy to think that if we just do a few things right, our kids will "get it" and succeed in life because they will learn from our mistakes and proceed as we would have done if only we'd known then what we know now. Right?

But these frustrations are predicated on the notion that our kids are like us. We presume that, once they possess the requisite facts, they will apply logic like we do and come to the same conclusions we do. We presume they are motivated by the same things that motivate us. Our differences make our lives richer, but they can also be frustrating sometimes.

Consider for a moment the textbook Bootstrap Patriarch (See Section 3.5.1 below). This person has built significant wealth from little or nothing, and usually is highly intelligent with a "Type A" personality. He often grew up in adverse conditions with an education that was average at best. There is no way to ensure that this person's child will be as intelligent as he or she is, or as outwardly motivated. But this Patriarch will typically try to give his child a "better" childhood, so the child will face less adversity growing up and, if possible, will attend better schools. Why in the world would anyone expect that these two people would turn out the same as adults?

Another important consideration is that we all change more over time than we realize. Things that were no big deal at one time can seem incredibly foolish in hindsight. Having a double standard is easy. As they say, wisdom comes from the kind of experience you get when you do foolish things. At some point, Patriarchs have to accept the consequences of their kids' mistakes. It's not easy. But if they can mitigate the damage done, the kids may come out better for it in the end.

3.3 Enfranchisement.

Enfranchisement generally means giving someone a vote or other privilege. In this book, it means the amount by which a Patriarch permits other family members to participate in the management of the family's Castle. Enfranchisement can be gradual or swift. A Patriarch can systematically and purposefully hand over responsibility in increments, or he can hand over the keys to the Castle and be done with it. Families are more likely to avoid the Family Power Vacuum if Patriarchs will enfranchise younger generations carefully over time.

Enfranchisement poses a major problem for most Patriarchs. Attorneys in the business of wealth transfer see this problem again and again. A client will come into a lawyer's office, perhaps with mild trepidation, but determined to establish a timeline for handing over the reins of the family business. The lawyer, in turn, formulates a technical, often tax-driven, plan of succession. The lawyer then sends a bill to the client, and maybe the plan works, maybe it doesn't.

In this scenario, the focus has been on the technical transfer of ownership and control of the business. Building your Castle requires a more holistic approach where, in addition to the technical matters, consideration is also given to the more abstract, subjective, and other intangible details that often make the difference between an effective power shift (one that avoids the Family Power Vacuum) and a Castle that goes up in flames.

The key concerns when addressing these intangibles are as follows:

3.3.1 Who to Enfranchise?

In medieval times, the rules of primogeniture dictated that the eldest living son would inherit a family's wealth. In modern times, notions of "fairness" generally dictate that inheritance should be equal at each successive generational level (called "*per stirpes*"). In many instances, however, and in particular where a family business is a Patriarch's primary asset, neither of these methods is particularly suitable. Rather, the Patriarch should identify who is best suited to take over the company and find happiness in life by continuing it as a successful operation. This may or may not be the eldest son. If even one of the kids lacks interest in the family business, foisting equal shares upon all of them is anything but fair.

3.3.2 When to Enfranchise?

The answer to this question is simple: The process should begin early and progress slowly, so it should take quite a while. Patriarchs are often loath to hand over power, so they wait too long to begin the process. When control does finally shift (often because something very bad has happened to the Patriarch), the transition is much too quick, so the successors don't have time to learn the business, and a Family Power Vacuum often results.

Instead, Patriarchs should begin training their family members on the family assets at an early age. The substantive process of enfranchisement in a family business should normally start when the kids reach adolescence. This does not mean that they should be invited to every board meeting. But why not have them work the mail room or answer the phones as a summer job in high school or college? Why not discuss strategic decisions at the dinner table? Are you thinking about buying a new machine or moving to a new office? Tell the kids and ask them what they think. You may like what you hear. Note that involvement early on will also help identify who should take over as various family members gravitate toward or away from the family business. You cannot distribute your assets fairly until you have this information.

A Patriarch must be patient, however. It can be tempting to hand over too much responsibility too quickly. Importantly, the family member taking over responsibility for something needs to be ready and interested in taking the new task on. I remember when my son was 7 and I tried to teach him to light a grill. Cooking is very important in our family and we grill a lot. He had always liked to watch me light the charcoal in our grill, so I thought he would like to become our family's "master of the flame." Over the course of several weeks, I tried to show him how to light the grill properly, but it never stuck. I finally accepted that he wasn't ready to take on this task and moved on. Maybe he'll come around eventually, or maybe he won't. The point is, I had to recognize that I was pushing this enfranchisement onto my son and he wasn't ready for it. The same thing applies in the context of a family business or other area. It's not enough for the

Patriarch to be ready to hand over some responsibility. The family member taking on that responsibility has to be ready for it as well.

3.3.3   How to Enfranchise?

Ideally, enfranchisement should take place in a series of small steps over many years or decades. As a young person, the family member is exposed to the business with a job that involves less significant, administrative work. He or she can answer phones, work the mail room, get coffee, or anything along those lines. That's the starting point. This is where the young family member learns about decorum and acceptable behavior, as well as work ethic. From that point, learning begins by osmosis. In college, the family member can intern. Later, he or she gets a junior office that fits his or her personality (sales, production, whatever). Next come introductions to clients and suppliers, then increasing managerial responsibility, executive status, and a seat on the board. The progress is slow but deliberate. This is Building your Castle.

With regard to the above example, a few notes apply. First, analogs to the example above can be identified for professional service businesses as well as for families whose primary business is managing their own assets. Second, the procedure should not be dictated by timing. One does not graduate to a senior office after surviving a year in the junior office. Instead, mastery of a given skill or position should be paramount, and a Patriarch should be willing to accept that a given family member may never rise above a given level. Third, by the time a second-generation family member (the

Patriarch's child) reaches executive status, his or her children (the Patriarch's grandchild) may already be entering the process themselves.

3.3.4 Why Enfranchise?

This question is really about keeping eyes on the ultimate goal of Building your Castle. The answer varies greatly from family to family and Patriarch to Patriarch. In the context of a family business, the answer may be that enfranchisement is necessary for the maintenance and continuation of the business. If the goal is to make the family as productive and happy as possible, and nobody in the family cares about the business, then perhaps enfranchisement in the business is less meaningful. In that case, perhaps the Patriarch should look for an exit strategy whereby the business can be liquidated and proceeds distributed. In such a case, enfranchisement may mean involving other family members in the management of investments after the business is liquidated.

In the context of managing family wealth, enfranchisement takes on a slightly different tone. In this regard, training younger generations in the proper custodianship of wealth is absolutely necessary. Failure to do this can be disastrous for a family. Enfranchising younger generations in the process of wealth management, on a limited scale, will often be the best way to accomplish this training.

The examples above may not be feasible for a given family but they represent ideals towards which a family might strive. Don't give up on Building your Castle just because your family does not fit perfectly within the lines of textbook examples. Find a Facilitator if you have to, and modify the parameters to fit your particular situation.

Similarly, don't beat yourself up because you didn't start talking to your kids about your company at age four or five. A late start is better than no start at all. Think about how you can adapt these principles to your particular family circumstances and go from there. You can only change the future, so there is no reason to look back. Finally, we get to a completely different arena of enfranchisement. This arena is the personal enfranchisement of family members in the family's own administration. In this sense, enfranchisement refers to the participation of various family members in Family Assemblies, on committees, or the like. Here, enfranchisement questions must be answered on a case-by-case basis because of the many variables involved. As a general rule, starting the enfranchisement process early is still a good idea. If a particular family member does not fit well into any of the defined roles within the family, make up a new one so the family member can participate and feel a sense of ownership within the family. More often than not, this will pay dividends in the future.

3.4 Communication.

A principal theme throughout this book is the benefit of effective communication. Communication is the elixir most prescribed against the plague of family discord. The costs and heartache of every single probate litigation matter that I've ever been involved with could have been significantly reduced, or avoided entirely, if a Patriarch had communicated effectively with all relevant parties. That may sound a little extreme, but I'm convinced it's true.

But not all communication is the same. The point of communicating is getting a meaningful message from one source to another. This involves countless variables, each of which may vary by degree. For example, communication always begins with a sender. The sender's ability to communicate may be good, bad, or something in-between. Next is the message itself. The message may be complex or simple, straightforward or nuanced. After that, consider the method of communication, which includes both language and some sort of medium by which the language is transferred. Finally, we get to the receiver, who like the sender, may be good or bad at communicating effectively.

Consider a baby communicating to its parent. The message may be as simple as, "Feed me," but effectively communicating that to the parent may be quite difficult. In that case, the sender is not a good communicator. To be sure, his or her blood-curdling cries relay the message that something is wrong, and the parent might logically narrow the message down to a few possibilities. The medium of communication—voice traveling through the air—is the simplest possible option, and the receiver is perfectly able to receive the message. Clearly, something is wrong. But one link in the chain is broken. The baby doesn't yet have a grasp of language, and this is enough to cause a systemic failure. The parent might eventually deduce through trial and error that the child is hungry, but the actual act of communication is a failure.

Although the above example is very simplistic, the same principles apply every time we communicate. In the context of intra-familial communication where emotional tensions can run high, the primary hurdle is nuance. Members of most families all speak a common language and are fully capable of transmitting words and phrases between themselves. But the meaning behind any of those words or phrases can change dramatically depending on time, place, context, and a whole host of other variables. In fact, this phenomenon is so prevalent that we, as a society, regularly make jokes about it. After all, every man knows what to say when his wife asks if a particular pair of jeans makes her butt look fat, right?

There are different personality types within families. Each of the family members can play a meaningful role within the family. Any of them can be leveraged to Build your Castle. To do that, however, family members must be accepted for who they are and enfranchised in a way that fits their personality. But you can't do either of those things unless you can communicate with them.

Communicating with family members necessarily means making some adjustments. Whether we realize it or not, most of us already do this regularly. Each of us adopts different speech patterns, mannerisms, sentence structure, and even accents around different groups, including family. A person might cuss like a sailor at work but speak like an angel in front of his or her grandmother.

This ability to adjust has important implications for Building your Castle. The way we communicate, even when we think we're being polite and straightforward, can be a turnoff, or it can be motivating, depending on who is receiving our messages. A successful Castle Builder learns to notice when another family member is being turned off and takes reasonable steps to first accept and then adapt to the other family member's needs. The real magic happens when the Castle Builder figures out how to turn the communication tables around and motivate other family members. This is enfranchisement. A Castle cannot be built by one person alone. It has to be done by the entire family, and that necessarily involves someone giving direction and guidance in a way that family members will get fired up about digging every trench, laying every stone, and painting every wall.

3.4.1 Misinterpretation.

On its face, misinterpretation is where a recipient receives a message that is materially different from the one sent, with neither party realizing it. As a general rule, interpretation is the prerogative of the sender, not the recipient, because the sender formulates the message. Because the sender has control over what is sent and how, it is primarily this person's responsibility to make sure the message is properly put together and transmitted. This means, when a message is misinterpreted, the blame lies with the message sender, not the recipient, most of the time. This rule is, of course, subject to a reasonableness standard, meaning that the recipient is expected to be reasonably equipped to receive the message intelligibly, and the recipient must also make reasonable efforts to interpret the message properly.

Misinterpretation is a real issue in the context of intra-family communication. Emotions can run high when you talk to other family members about Building your

Castle. Also, the people communicating with each other can often have different perspectives. Consider, for example, a discussion between mother, Mildred, and son, Sam, about family wealth. If Mildred earned and accumulated that wealth through hard work before Sam was born, she will have a hard time explaining to him how difficult her life was before he was born. If Sam has never lived without wealth, how can he possibly be expected to understand what life is like without it? It's Mildred's responsibility to understand Sam's lack of experience and make accommodations to get her intended messages through to her son.

Misinterpretation can happen in one of two ways: Either the substance of the intended communication or the underlying subtext can be lost. And the latter can happen at varying levels. Over 80% of human communication is nonverbal, and this includes subtext. Suppose Mildred from the example above is communicating to Sam about the family's finances. Suppose Mildred discloses the value of a given brokerage account. Sam might simply misunderstand the number. Perhaps he transposed two digits in his head or heard Mildred say "nine" instead of "five." That's a substantive misinterpretation. On the other hand, the subtext of the message might be lost if Sam fails to grasp the meaning of the number in the greater context. For example, does that number make Mildred rich or poor? A deeper subtext might be the emotional tone that Sam perceives. Is Mildred happy about this number? Is Mildred mad at Sam about something? These cues are much harder to deal with, but it is still Mildred's responsibility to deliver the message in a way that Sam can reasonably understand.

Fortunately, there are several tricks to minimize misinterpretation. The first is simply to communicate frequently. Practice does, in fact, make perfect in this area. Another trick is to simply be aware of the potential problem. Just thinking about a problem like this ahead of time will make you better at addressing it in the moment. In the military, they do exactly this. When radio operators speak to each other they use universal words instead of letters (Alpha, Bravo, Charlie, etc.) because they anticipate and work around the potential problem of understanding another person over the radio. Sometimes, asking a recipient to repeat back a communication is even worthwhile, so the sender can know it was properly received. Psychologists use this trick in therapy all the time. It's a great way to sift through both substantive details as well as subtext.

Watch out for exaggeration, including theatrics and superlatives. Some people do this because they overcorrect and take things to an extreme. Others do it because they crave attention. Still others do it because they don't (or can't) understand a situation well enough to converse at the proper level. Either way, it's indicative of some other problem and off-putting in its own right. But correcting a communicator who exaggerates is difficult. The best you can do is lead by example. Try to model proper behavior and get the person to notice how you handle a given situation. It may help to point out privately how much you'd like to say but don't. It may also help to call someone out on an exaggeration, for example, by asking for specifics. If you choose this tactic, take care to make your inquiry nonthreatening.

3.5 The Mad Hatters.

In law, we often refer to the various "hats" that people wear. For example, if a person is both a beneficiary and a trustee of a trust, we would say that he has one set of rights when he's wearing his trustee hat and another when he's wearing his beneficiary hat. Similarly, in the old days, various people could be distinguished by the hats they wore. A priest might have one hat, while a huntsman had another. The same applies in families today. Each of us holds a different role in our family depending on our personality and station. Understanding these hats can help us all communicate better.

The remainder of this chapter discusses some of the more common character types that frequently appear in the context of Building your Castle. It's important to understand that these characters are archetypal generalizations. They are not meant as a perfect description of any one individual. Also, the characters often overlap in the real world. They are not exclusive. Many people will fit into more than one category below, but thinking about each, in turn, may be valuable to all your family members.

3.5.1 Patriarch.

We've spoken quite a bit about Patriarchs already, but for the most part, we've done so from the Patriarch's perspective. This section is addressed to family members who are not Patriarchs.

Personalities are not static. This holds true for Patriarchs just like everyone else. But because the Patriarch serves as the chief provider of security and stability, changes in his or her personality are harder to accept. Building your Castle means understanding this and thinking ahead to mitigate potential problems that might arise. What will happen if the Patriarch becomes more cautious and slows down? What will happen if the Patriarch outlives all of his or her friends? What will happen if the Patriarch outlives his money?

Patriarchs generally come in two flavors. "**Bootstrappers**" have lifted themselves up by their own bootstraps and have often amassed their wealth out of very little or nothing. Professional advisors refer to the other flavor of Patriarch as belonging to the "**Lucky Sperm Club**" because they were born into their wealth. Both flavors, however, present issues which can be addressed effectively with a little forethought and understanding.

In one form or another, stability is the Patriarch's primary concern and motivation. For a significant period of their lives, Patriarchs busy themselves (often to a fault) with their own establishment. In this phase, they either build their wealth (in the case of a Bootstrapper) or augment it (in the case of the Lucky Sperm Club). Either way, this phase is about financial growth.

But at some point, nearly all Patriarchs exit the growth phase. They go from being wealth creators to either wealth distributors or sometimes wealth hoarders. The psychology behind this phenomenon is extremely complex and woefully understudied. But its effect is profound because families, much like any other economic system, flourish in times of growth and wither in times of stagnation. When the driving force behind the family's preeminence starts to falter, the entire family follows suit. Unfortunately, most families don't recognize this change until their downfall is already well underway.

Sometimes, the end of a growth phase may be brought on suddenly by some catastrophic event. Such an event may even be strong enough to trigger the Family Power Vacuum. More often than not, this period doesn't just end rapidly. It peters out over time, leaving the family to languish. This slow letdown is also very difficult to detect.

If you throw a frog into hot water, it will jump out and save itself. But if you put a frog in tepid water and slowly raise the temperature, it will stay there until it cooks and dies. Families tend to act the same way, and they suffer dire consequences if this goes on for too long.

To make matters worse, Patriarchs will frequently engage in increasingly destructive behavior as they begin to see the handwriting on the wall. They will often neglect investments because they are too frightened of losing ground and simply lack the energy it takes to make sound investment decisions. On the other hand, in an effort to maintain the illusion of continued economic success, Patriarchs will continue living lavishly and supporting dependent family members.

Fortunately, there is some good news. Families that are Building their Castle deploy two key strategies to avoid these problems. The first is simply being aware of the problem and the potential dangers. Just like the old G.I. Joe public service announcements used to say, "Knowing is half the battle."

The second tool is the basis of this book. By leveraging well-prepared and educated human capital within the family, it is possible to transition control of family assets from the Patriarch to other family members so that they can enter into a new growth phase on their own. This will minimize the peaks and valleys families experience as successive Patriarchs assume control, hit their stride, peak, and then slow down.

Note that nothing in this section has anything to do with the personal respect that is properly due a Patriarch. Where an individual has been an effective builder and/or steward of wealth, he deserves respect for his service until his dying day and beyond. Indeed, relinquishing control of family wealth in a timely and effective manner should engender that much more respect. Patriarchs and other family members alike would do well to keep this in mind.

3.5.2 Coastal.

A "**Coastal**" child is often portrayed as a family's success story. He or she has grown up, done well, avoided trouble, and moved to the coast for college or first job. He or she is on the rise and, more likely than not, following a well-planned trajectory. These are the kids we tell people about. And they know it.

Coastal children display a few stereotypical characteristics. They often make significant incomes. As such, they can often be the ones who take on the financial responsibility of assisting with family matters. On the other hand, they tend to lead highly stressful lives that don't afford much time for family. Other than a trip home for the holidays every so often, they don't tend to come back home very much. For this reason, they are usually not the best choice for the role of Caregiver (see below). Depending on the situation, however, they may be well suited to act in advisory or fiduciary roles that may be performed remotely. Thus, Coastal children may be a good choice for positions like trustee or guardian of the estate, and they might also be productive on a trust committee or family council.

Conflicts can arise between Coastal children and other family members. For one thing, Coastals often have unrealistic expectations. Most Coastal children spend a lot of time around highly intelligent, highly driven people in a cutthroat, fast-paced, and active environment. A major challenge for these people is dealing with the pace of life at home. This problem is compounded in the family setting where jealousy, entitlement, and other destructive emotions run high. Other family members may try to get ahead of this stress trigger before it causes their Coastal child or sibling to blow a proverbial gasket. Similarly, if you're the Coastal, then you need to try not to be stressed out by these potential triggers. Patience, as they say, is a virtue.

Of course, the reverse is also true. When a Coastal child comes home to participate in a family event, whether it's a wedding, funeral, holiday, Family Assembly, or what have you, he will engender anxiety in other family members when he brings his torrent of high energy with him. If he is constantly on the phone and complaining about the bad Wi-Fi, other family members may label him a jerk. And rightly so. To the extent they seek to one day assume the role of Patriarch themselves, Coastal family members are well advised to remember that family activities are, first and foremost, about family.

One very interesting phenomenon displayed by Coastal children is that they tend to come home eventually. Often, the very factors that make life attractive to young, hard-charging adults become unattractive when it's time to settle down and start a family, so a child who goes off to seek his fortune in New York at age 22 may return at age 35 with a spouse and small baby in tow, particularly if home is a major metropolitan area with good job prospects. When this happens, however, that hard-charging, driven personality is not likely to disappear quickly.

If Patriarchs over-involve anyone, it's their Coastal children. They think of them as "the best" and mistakenly assume this means they are the best at everything. Patriarchs seldom stop to think about what their Coastal children are good at, or even allow themselves the thought that those children might be no good at all when it comes to certain areas that might not come up at the country club Gin Rummy table. But you can't Build your Castle out of towers only. You need walls and ditches and privies and larders too.

The Coastal child's primary motivation is progress. Stagnation is anathema. If you want to keep a Coastal family member happy, show him the plan (or better, let him think he came up with the plan), and then show him how it's being implemented.

The Coastal child's primary fear is lack of information. Because this person is far away most of the time, he may feel out of the loop on family affairs. If a lack of information induces fear or resentment in the Coastal family member, then he may react irrationally. Consider, for example, the case where Coastal sibling, Craig, believes his sister, Sandra, back at home is exerting undue influence on the Patriarch, Peter, to make a change in Peter's estate plan. Although there may have been a very good reason for the change to Peter's estate plan, it was not communicated effectively to Craig, and he let things stew in his head until he finally decided to lawyer up and investigate formally. Even in a reasonably best-case scenario, that's a 5- or 6-figure error by Sandra, and in many cases, Craig is the only one who can actually foot the legal bill.

The Coastal family member's Achilles heel is apathy and self-importance. If the Coastal family member is too busy to plug in with the family or just doesn't care to make time to do so, then there is little the family can do. Obviously, a person like this should not be named to any critical roles within the family system. The family should keep in mind, however, that a person's apathy can often change on a dime, so the family should do what it can to keep the lines of communication open.

3.5.3 Cassandra.

In Greek mythology, Cassandra was the daughter of King Priam and Queen Hecuba, the rulers of Troy. As the story goes, the god Apollo tried to seduce Cassandra by giving her the power of prophecy. But she refused him. Enraged, Apollo spat in Cassandra's mouth, cursing her with the inability to persuade anyone of the future she saw. Cassandra predicted all the important events of the Trojan war, including her family's ultimate defeat, but nobody believed her. Instead, they said she was mad and locked her in a tower.

Nearly every family has a "**Cassandra.**" You may not realize it, though, because it may not be outwardly apparent. If you can imagine what it might feel like to be cursed like the mythic figure, you may be able to spot the person in your family that feels the same way. The Cassandra is often an outcast in his family. This person doesn't need to be told to think outside the box because he probably doesn't acknowledge the box in the first place. Cassandras may be introverted or extroverted.

A Cassandra is usually studious, but lacks confidence. They are easily distracted and may go off on a tangent. Cassandras appreciate creativity and art. A Cassandra often moves through the world in fits and spurts. A person like this may seem to have her head in the clouds one minute and then say something brilliant the next. In fact, she may have some of the best strategic thinking skills in the family, so she may come up with some of the best ideas. But you will often have to sift through a number of bad ideas before you find the good ones.

To effectively Build your Castle, you have to be able to harness and leverage the talents of your various family members on a subconscious and emotional level. No archetypal family member makes this clearer than a Cassandra. If you think you have a Cassandra in your family, you may want to try sending some motivational cues to see if you get a response. Take the time to listen to and compliment something analytical the suspected Cassandra says, or point out a time when she was right and you were wrong. If you get a positive response, you may have found your Cassandra.

A Cassandra is usually self-motivated by knowledge and learning. This too may be difficult to spot, however, because the way a Cassandra might go about seeking knowledge, as well as the actual information sought, may be nontraditional. A Cassandra might be a connoisseur, expert, or hobbyist in some obscure area. Don't hold this against her.

Often, a Cassandra wants to participate meaningfully in the family business without taking on the extra responsibilities of Patriarch. Generally speaking, the more specialized that participation, the better, but you want to avoid a level of specialization that ostracizes this person. A Cassandra might fit in well as the family company's web designer, but don't limit her role to a part of the website that nobody uses or looks at, like the terms and conditions page.

The Achilles heel of a Cassandra is poor communication and an inability to get things done. Cassandras are often frustrated by the minutia involved with a given task and this slows them down. They often lack the ability to sift through the information at hand to process the important bits. This is why they are so long-winded and slow.

3.5.4 Eldest Son.

Primogeniture is the right by which the eldest child (usually, the eldest son) inherits the parents' property. Although old-fashioned, it nonetheless survives, both formally and informally. The British monarchy follows these rules and for a long time, they were followed this side of the pond as well. But for obvious reasons, the Founding Fathers—most pronouncedly, Thomas Jefferson—looked on primogeniture with disdain, so it was excluded from the law of the fledgling United States.

In the U.S., we typically favor equal distribution of assets among family lines. This is known as "*per stirpital*" distribution. Most Wills in the U.S. provide that some or all distributions of a person's property are to go to their descendants "*per stirpes*." (Interestingly, Winston Churchill is said to have referred to this preference as the "Spanish Curse" because of the way it dilutes family assets along family branches instead of concentrating them in a direct line.)

While there is no formal or legal impact to birth order anymore in this country, that doesn't mean certain individuals don't feel that there ought to be. "**Eldest Sons**" (who, just to be clear, can be sons or daughters nowadays) are characterized by a sense of entitlement, jealousy, and pride. On the other hand, they may also be protective, welcoming, and supporting. Eldest Sons often expect they will be Patriarch of the family someday.

As a character type, Eldest Sons are almost always the oldest of several siblings. But not all such siblings are Eldest Sons. Families can have multiple children but no Eldest Son as described in this book, so the trick is figuring out whether the oldest person among several siblings fits the mold. Anecdotally, it does seem that the more children a family has, the more likely it is for an Eldest Son to manifest. Eldest Sons also tend to appear more frequently where siblings are not close together in age.

The Eldest Son differs from the Coastal child because the Eldest Son feels his entitlement to be intrinsic. "I should get the keys to the Castle because I'm the oldest." That's the only justification they need. Coastals, on the other hand, feel that they should be in charge because they've earned it somehow. The fact that what they've actually earned—say a master's in Economics from a top-tier business school—has nothing to do with Building a Castle, doesn't come into play.

As with all personality types, families should identify this archetype and leverage its benefits. Fortunately, this is not at all difficult to do (at least in the short-run) because the Eldest Son's motivation is so clear. This person wants to be Patriarch, and he will typically be enthusiastic about anything he perceives as advancing towards that goal.

While Coastal children often move to far-away cities because they need to go out and make their fortunes,

Eldest Sons feel the need to stay at home so they can keep an eye on the family fortune they expect to one day inherit. These are fundamentally different perspectives, and it will behoove other family members to take note of each.

A major problem with the Eldest Son mentality is that it's a double-edged sword. A large part of an Eldest Son's entitlement might come from the way he or she is treated by others. When estate planning attorneys ask their clients who they'd like to name to positions such as executor, trustee, attorney-in-fact, and the like, it is very common for parents to name their children in age order. Why? It may only be an easy way to make an otherwise difficult decision. But it begs the question: What other decisions were made in this manner over time? What cues have the Eldest Sons (and their other siblings) been given over time that reinforce this stereotype?

To the extent a Patriarch intends to give the keys to the Castle to an Eldest Son, so be it. A family is less likely to run into the Family Power Vacuum where the estate plan meets everyone's expectations. However, a person who has been treated as an Eldest Son all his life is bound to be sorely upset when he runs headlong and completely unexpectedly into that Spanish Curse. And what do people do when they get upset? They act irrationally and cause damage.

3.5.5 The Wanderer.

Perhaps the most difficult people to deal with in families are those that fit into a personality type that we'll call the "**Wanderer**." As the name implies, Wanderers tend to travel. They travel the world, looking for fulfillment and contentment that is not available at home. Because they can't find what they need at home, they are especially hard to motivate. Patriarchs are lords of their Castles because they have mastered the world around them. Each is familiar with the trappings, customs, and circumstances of his or her particular location. But many Patriarchs have a limited skillset. They may be successful at home, but that doesn't mean they understand everything the world has to offer. Thus, when the Wanderer realizes his or her needs are not being met at home, the Patriarch may not know how to help. A Wanderer's need goes beyond the mere desire to go on walkabout. A Wanderer travels compulsively over the long-term, and his disassociation with home can cause frustration in the Patriarch. This frustration, which may be compounded by a Wanderer's inability to effectively convey his or her needs, can turn into animosity.

Some Wanderers wander because they sense a void in their lives which they want to fill. Wandering is often a spiritual endeavor. Most Wanderers seek some sort of spiritual enlightenment. Sometimes, they reject Western culture and seek fulfillment in various Eastern traditions. Sometimes, they are extreme adrenaline junkies seeking thrills. Sometimes, the Wanderer's need is purely a call for attention. Daddy is big and important and rich. People pay attention to him. I'm going to make people pay attention to me by spending a bunch of money all over the world. Of course, this concept is really about validation.

Many Wanderers affirmatively seek to escape something from home. These people have been hurt in some way, either by their families directly or because their families failed to protect them from some outside force, and they want to get away from that pain. These Wanderers may join the military or seek personal relationships in far-away places.

Wanderers generally suffer from jealousy, shame, and low self-esteem. They have always lived in their Patriarch's shadow so they don't understand how to judge their own self-worth. Despite their best efforts, they have not found their own success (as it is defined at home), and they are jealous their Patriarch has found that success. Rightly or wrongly, Wanderers often feel they are unloved.

If there is one thing Wanderers really like to do (besides wander) it's talk. They like to talk about the things they've seen, the people they've met, the enlightenment they have found, and the fun they've had. To combat their unhappy feelings and motivate them to participate in Building the family's Castle, Wanderers can be given a voice. Let them tell their story. Let them show the family what they have learned in their travels. Validate that experience without being patronizing and give them honest thanks for broadening the family's horizons. The trick is to do this without showing favoritism over other family members.

To be clear, not all people who like to travel are Wanderers. Nor do all Wanderers travel. Indeed, some

Wanderers merely move back and forth across the social spectrum. And it is certainly enlightening for young people to get out to see the world. Building your Castle means being attuned to the possibility that someone in your family might be a Wanderer. If this is the case, it may behoove you to discover why this person wanders.

You do not need to "fix" a Wanderer. They are often perfectly capable of leading meaningful, if not productive, lives on their own. You can and should accept them for who they are. But you may be able to benefit the whole family by getting to know them a little bit better.

3.5.6 Black Sheep.

Family members who we might refer to as "**Black Sheep**" are far more pervasive than most people realize. Nearly all of us have one, but most of us think nobody else does. If you happen to have a family without a Black Sheep, one of three things is true: Either 1) you should thank your lucky stars that you get to have that one-in-a-million "unicorn family"; 2) your family is very small; or 3) your family actually does have a Black Sheep, but you don't know it because the Black Sheep is you.

Black Sheep may be characterized in a number of ways. At one end of the spectrum, they might simply be shy or lack clear motivation. If they are a little too comfortable with Mommy or Daddy, they may never leave home and thus fail to launch. At the other end of the spectrum, they may suffer from an array of debilitating conditions which may be naturally occurring, the result of some accident, self-inflicted, or some combination of the three. At the latter end of this spectrum, a family member's special needs will dictate much of how the family interacts with them.

It may seem cruel to group family members with special needs under the auspice of Black Sheep, which may connote some sort of willfulness. But the simple reason for this is pragmatism. It doesn't matter if a condition is self-inflicted or naturally occurring. In either case, additional family resources will be expended dealing with such people, which may generate jealousies among other family members.

There are seldom any "right" answers when Black Sheep are concerned. There is no playbook because each condition is different, as is each individual. If you add in the complexity of changing moral imperatives and social norms, the situation can get complicated very quickly. Not long ago a gay sibling would have been universally looked on as a Black Sheep. Not anymore. Indeed, the Black Sheep in most families now is *that uncle* (it seems) who can't accept the gay family member.

It is the very nature of family, if not its primary purpose, that we care for our own, especially when they are weak, feeble, and unable to reciprocate our compassion. But what is a family to do when something impairs a family member's ability to function productively in society? Where the problem is naturally occurring, as is the case with a disease or mental illness, it may seem easy to jump to the conclusion that no amount of care, love, and attention could possibly be too much.

And yet there are numerous incidents where an affliction, particular one impacting a young child, has caused families to break up. In one such instance, a young child was diagnosed with cancer. The medical bills for treating the cancer depleted the family's finances. The mother and father spent so much time caring for their sick child that they neglected their marriage and their other child. Although the sick child was eventually healed, the parents divorced, and the sibling was a full-fledged alcoholic before finishing college.

Two lessons may be derived from this tragic story: First, family members have to take care of themselves too. This lesson is the same one we're taught every time we get on an airplane. Secure your own oxygen mask first, then assist others with theirs. This strategy may result in the other person passing out for a second, but then you can get his mask on and revive him. Conversely, if you try to do things the other way around, you might get the other person's mask on and save him but he will be unable to help you, so at best you will die. At worst, you will both die.

The second lesson is that the Patriarch and other family members need to be vigilant. If certain members within the family are dealing with a Black Sheep (for example, children dealing with a Black Sheep grandchild), the rest of the family should come to the aid of the caregiving family members. Remember that it can be hard to ask for help, so just offer it. Taking care of your sick grandkid every so often so your son can go on a date night with his wife is going to be a lot easier than taking care of your son when he divorces. Not to mention taking care of your successful business when your ex-daughter-in-law is trying to pry half of your son's share away from him. The same rule applies if the sick child is a niece or a nephew instead of a grandchild. And don't forget about the siblings of the afflicted family member. Particularly during their formative years, you can do a world of good for them and your family as a whole, if you step in and pay them some attention. Note that, for this purpose, giving people money does not count. The family members may need financial support, and you might give it to them, but that doesn't take the place of moral and emotional support.

On the other hand, the sentimentality may be very different where the Black Sheep's affliction is (at least ostensibly) self-inflicted. This may be the case where a family member suffers from addiction, or he may struggle financially because he never graduated from college. Maybe she got pregnant young and had to enter the workforce to support the child. Maybe he made a bad career move or investment and never managed to recover. Whatever the cause, the family is duty-bound to provide some reasonable form of assistance. Of course, the issue always turns on what is reasonable, and this must be determined on a case-by-case basis.

Fortunately, we can look to some generalizations for assistance. First, we know we must provide some, but not unlimited assistance. Where assistance is easily rendered, it should be offered. At the other end of the spectrum, however, it is not reasonable to subject yourself to real threat of violence or bodily harm. Nor must you cause yourself great financial harm in the care of family members (although many will do this anyway). Within these two bounds lie a number of options which are all dependent on the facts and circumstances of a given case. Sometimes, generosity will be appropriate and other times, tough love may be the better approach.

Another thing to keep in mind is that nearly all Black Sheep are motivated by fear. Usually, this fear centers around preserving the *status quo*. Children come home from college and live in the basement for years because it's comfortable for them. It gives them something they can hold onto and depend on. People in this situation can easily get stuck in a rut.

If the Black Sheep is an addict, his fear is chemically amplified. As is always the case with fear, this will generally lead to irrational behavior. For example, in one case I worked on, an adult child returned to live with his parents after a failed business venture. The child was an alcoholic and was unable to secure any meaningful work. He was so scared of being forced out that he turned his fear onto his parents. Every time they asked him to move out, he threatened to commit suicide. Although hardly a congenial relationship, this went on for some ten years.

The first step in addressing this irrational behavior is to make yourself and others aware of it. Next, the family must come together and develop a plan for dealing with it. This may be something as simple as withholding more than *de minimis* amounts of cash, so the person doesn't ever have enough money to buy drugs, or it may be as complicated as a full-fledged intervention.

When assessing the reasonableness of care given to a Black Sheep, it can help to disassociate the thinking from the family. The goal of this is to trick your mind into forgetting about the emotional baggage that goes with family generally and Black Sheep in particular. Create a hypothetical scenario in your head or a discussion setting where another family is going through a similar situation. What would you, as an outsider expect them to do for their Black Sheep? What are the parameters that would cause you to feel differently? How would you judge that hypothetical family? If you're really stuck on how to deal with a Black Sheep in the family, try this technique and see if it doesn't break the stalemate.

Many clients ask when it is appropriate to cut off their kids (or cut them out of the estate plan). For the most part, the legal answer is that clients may cut off their kids whenever they want to. There are a few states (Louisiana is one) with laws on the books that limit this, but in most states, it's completely allowable. Parents have a general duty to support their children through high school, and they must allow their children to remain on their health insurance until age 26. But otherwise, parents are free to cut their kids off whenever they want.

The second answer is more practical in nature. If you cut a child off, or take them out of your estate plan, be ready for a legal battle. You may also need to prepare your other children for a legal battle. Typically, weaning children off of your financial support is much more manageable than simply cutting everything off at once—particularly when the decision to do that is made in the context of a heated argument. On the other hand, cutting someone off cold turkey is much more assertive and may lead to quick changes for the better. If a person is weaned slowly, he may develop bad habits as he slowly adapts to a new life. Building your Castle is hard.

The third and final answer is a moral one. Finally, from a moral standpoint, your obligation to your kids lasts for your mutual lives. There may be something to the notion that, by withdrawing financial support, you are actually promoting their continued growth and maturity. Many birds, after all, have to be pushed from their nest before they will learn to fly. Fair enough. But the familial connection should never be broken without good reason. If a person is physically abusive, or severely emotionally abusive, severing ties may be unavoidable. Short of this, however, the bond should not be broken, even if it takes work to keep the connection. That's Building your Castle.

A few final comments are worth noting regarding failures to launch. There are many examples where children have failed to launch because they have been enabled by their parents. Sometimes, this can be as simple as a well-meaning parent trying to help his or her kid out. Other times, unhealthy, often subconscious, desires may lead the parent to keep the child too near for too long, such that he or she fails to join ranks when the rest of his or her age group marches into independence.

This problem tends to build slowly because its beginnings can come about so innocently: The child comes back from college for a few weeks while he looks for a job. But before you know it, years have passed and the child is still delivering pizzas and sleeping in the basement.

Fortunately, there are a number of ways to address this situation. The child's motivation may show as a litmus test. Is the child making any attempt to move forward, or are they truly stagnating? Many children in this scenario will stagnate. And why not? Their basic needs are provided, and from their perspective, even if all isn't well, it's at least tolerable. As a result, they do nothing.

In instances where this is the case, action is needed from the parents to persuade the child to start down his own path. Most people know this, but they tend to apply it sporadically and harshly. Perhaps an argument develops, and the parents finally lay down an ultimatum. While this approach may be necessary in extreme circumstances, it can often backfire.

The better approach may be to seek alternative avenues that might catch the child's attention and motivate him to get his life started. This approach is a great opportunity for other family members to get involved and make suggestions. Sometimes, a child is more willing to listen to people who aren't the mother or father.

Where motivation is present, however, letting children blossom on their own and at their own pace may be wisest. Consider the unlikely story of the young man who partied a little too much in college and failed to land a job. He went back to his parents' place. He smoked a lot of pot for a while, but eventually he decided to get his real estate license. It took him more than ten tries to pass the real estate exam, but he finally did it and eventually opened up his own real estate business. Within a decade of selling his first house, he had a multi-million-dollar business. Sometimes a kid just needs a little time to mature, so family members should not be too quick to jump to conclusions or decisions.

3.5.7 Caregiver/Responsible Party.

Baby Boomers are sometimes described as the "Sandwich Generation" because so many of them have been stuck between two generations that they are caring for at once. On the one side are their children, which were discussed in the previous section. On the other side are their parents. The number of adults caring for at least one parent has increased precipitously in recent years. The simple fact is that modern medicine has gotten very good at keeping us alive, but it can't (or won't) get very good at keeping us healthy, particularly when it comes to mental health. As a result, most of us will spend years of our lives unable to provide ourselves with even the most basic elements of care. These elements are known as "activities of daily living." They include things like bathing, eating, dressing, going to the bathroom, moving about, and the like.

As the saying goes, be nice to your kids because they get to pick your nursing home. For many, this isn't a joke at all. If you are a Patriarch, however, and you have the capacity to make your own decisions, this is something you need to think about very carefully. Odds are, your time will come too. It's best to prepare for it.

Legally, we prepare for the incapacity that inevitably finds those who live long enough by preparing certain documents that, for the most part, put the people we chose in control of us and our assets. These documents can also instruct our doctors and loved ones on what to do when the end is near. Everyone should get a competent and experienced lawyer to help put together a Comprehensive Estate Plan. But this alone is not Building your Castle.

Building your Castle means you go a step further. Not only do you draft the proper legal documents, but you also communicate directly with the people named in those documents and everyone else in your family about your decisions and wishes. This discussion can be a little uncomfortable, but it will save your family a tremendous amount of heartache. Even if your family is not headed for the Family Power Vacuum, the peace of mind they'll have knowing what to do when you can no longer guide them will be tremendously valuable.

When you speak with your family, you will appoint one or more people to take point, so to speak, with regard to your personal wellbeing as well as your finances. The first of these people is referred to in this book as your "**Caregiver**." A Caregiver may care for someone at home or in an eldercare facility (in which case she might be known as a "responsible party"). Generally, eldercare facilities want to deal with only one person, not a group of family members who might send mixed signals. This is something I learned the hard way when I was my family's Caregiver.

Caregivers are almost always family members. Caregivers may hire helpers, such as nurses or "granny sitters" to actually provide the care, but these are merely proxies of the Caregiver. Occasionally, a professional guardian or other outside party will be a person's Caregiver, but that almost always happens when there is no family available to the person under care.

Most caregivers are motivated by their sense of duty. They may also be motivated financially. That is fine, so long as the motivation is properly authorized, transparent to all the family members, and not subversive in any other way. Many Caregivers make great personal sacrifices to provide care to someone else. Their careers and personal lives can suffer significantly during the period in which they act in this role. For this reason, it is only right to compensate Caregivers for their time, particularly when there are plenty of assets available. Typically, this compensation will be based on an hourly rate, so it is important that the Caregiver keep good records to substantiate any compensation taken.

Of course, some Caregivers have ulterior financial motives. Sometimes, they will try to take advantage of the person being cared for. This is obviously immoral and completely wrong. The first red flag in this regard should be transparency and information flow. If the Caregiver refuses to provide detailed updates on the nature of the care and compensation received, something fishy is likely going on. Another red flag is where the Caregiver refuses to allow other family members access to the person being cared for.

3.5.8 Fiduciary.

The word "fiduciary" comes from the Latin *fidere*, which means "to trust." In modern terms, a fiduciary is a person trusted to care for another's assets. A fiduciary duty is the highest duty known to the law. In fact, it's higher than the duty a parent owes his or her child or that spouses owe each other. If you are a fiduciary, some very special, and often draconian, rules apply to you.

In this Book, the "**Fiduciary**" is the analogue of the Caregiver, just on the financial side. This is the person that writes checks for you when you can't do it for yourself or just don't want to. A Fiduciary might act under a power of attorney and/or as trustee of a trust. A Fiduciary might also be a guardian, but guardianship is generally something to be avoided if at all possible because it's very expensive, restrictive, and public.

Third-party Fiduciaries are much more common than outside Caregivers. Banks will often serve in the roles of trustee or estate administrator. Sometimes, a family's attorney will act as Fiduciary in one capacity or another. I have also seen several families avoid the Family Power Vacuum because a decedent named a trusted friend to be Fiduciary rather than a preferred child. Doing this can have two very potent psychological benefits. First, family members are much more likely to squabble amongst themselves. When an outsider is in control of an estate or trust, attitudes tend to remain much more professional. Second, when you appoint a family member to a fiduciary role, you paint a legal target on their back. In the right circumstances, it can be very helpful to let an outsider be the family's fall guy. This way the family is unified, albeit against the third-party, and not fighting internally.

As with Caregivers, your lawyer should help you with some documents to empower a Fiduciary to work for you. Once again, simply getting the legal documents drafted is not Building your Castle. To Build your Castle, you need to communicate with your family about who you want your Fiduciary to be, and who you *don't* want acting in that role. You also need to discuss with your family how you want your Fiduciary to operate. For example, should he make gifts to other family members with your assets? You should also be clear about how much control you want your fiduciary to have over your assets. You may want one person (or group of people) managing the assets, and another actually writing the checks to pay your bills. The best way to do this is simply to run through some hypothetical scenarios with your family and document those discussions.

Choosing a Fiduciary is a difficult task. First and foremost, you need to pick someone who is trustworthy.

The Fiduciary will face a lot of temptation, so you need someone who is not going to steal your money. You also want to pick someone who is meticulous, organized, and detail-oriented. Good Fiduciaries are also willing to seek guidance. They should not be overconfident people who think they know better already.

Perhaps above all, Fiduciaries need to be fanatical about recordkeeping and organization so that they can communicate with the various family members. They need to have systems for keeping documents and other information such that it can be easily accessed, both by them and by their successors.

When you choose your Fiduciary, you should set clear expectations with the entire family as to how the Fiduciary will communicate with them. For example, should the Fiduciary provide regular reports to the family? When the other family members don't get any information about how the Fiduciary is managing your financial affairs, they may get worried and act irrationally. Information sharing also has the benefit of keeping Fiduciaries on the straight and narrow. Fiduciaries are much less likely to do something they shouldn't if they know they have to tell their siblings about it.

Being a Fiduciary is hard work, so be sure to authorize yours to be compensated for the work he or she does. This authorization may have to be explicit in your legal documents. If so, make sure your lawyer covers it when the documents are drafted. The rules that apply to the financial motivation of Caregivers described above (good and bad) also apply to Fiduciaries.

Fiduciaries are motivated by fear. At least, they should be. Fiduciary litigation is big business for plaintiff's attorneys. Not only is the bar set very high to begin with, but most people are improperly educated on how to act as a Fiduciary, so they screw it up inadvertently. Think of it this way: How organized is your personal financial life? Are all your records meticulously filed? Do you pay each and every bill on time? Have all of your investment decisions been prudent? Probably not. If you're a Fiduciary, you're required to do all of these things or face the consequences. The role should not be underestimated. Most people who get sued for breach of a fiduciary duty have meant well, but failed nonetheless

3.5.9 Stepmothers.

Blended families make it much harder to Build your Castle and avoid the Family Power Vacuum. In the popular vernacular, we often refer to "evil" or "wicked" stepmothers. Since women tend to outlive men (and maybe also because some men tend to marry younger as they themselves get older), I refer to stepparents generally as "**Stepmothers**" in this book, even if it's not the most politically correct thing to do. Of course, all the issues described in this section apply equally to stepparents of both sexes.

The issue with Stepmothers is simple to understand but difficult to fix. Kids tend not to get along with Stepmothers as well as their fathers do. Most Patriarchs want to provide for their spouses, but to the extent the Patriarch's children are not also the Stepmother's children, they will view the Stepmother as a drag on their inheritance. The Stepmother not only spends down the kids' inheritance, she may also significantly delay that inheritance. She may be the same age as the kids, and if they have to wait for her to die before they can inherit the Patriarch's assets, they may never see their inheritance. If the Patriarch has children with the Stepmother, the problems get compounded.

Most Patriarchs try to find some sort of balance between the interests of their spouses and those of their children. Others take a hardline approach and simply put their spouse's interests first. To them, the assets are a windfall anyway, so the kids should worry about making their own fortunes. Only a few Patriarchs put their kids' interests ahead of their spouse's. This generally happens when both the Patriarch and the Stepmother have significant assets or when the Patriarch and stepparent marry late in life.

Exactly where a Patriarch lands on this spectrum is not particularly important. Stepmothers are usually motivated by fear because they worry that, once the Patriarch is gone, they will lose their support. The key is managing the expectations of the other family members. If the Patriarch wants to give all of his assets to the Stepmother outright, then he should tell the family. If the Patriarch wants to set up a trust so the Stepmother is provided for, but the assets are ultimately directed towards the kids, then that should be explained as well. It's interesting, though, how the Patriarch almost never wants to hold this conversation.

If you are the Stepmother in your family, be mindful of the emotional underpinnings of your relationship with your spouse's children. They may resent you for what your husband did to their mother. They may view you as an outsider or imposter. They may view you as the thing that stands between them and the inheritance they were promised. They may harbor one or all of these resentments without even realizing it.

3.5.10 Sheriff.

We have already mentioned Sheriffs briefly above in Chapter 1. Many Sheriffs are also a Coastal or a First Son. A Sheriff will try to assume power or exert influence, often in the Patriarch's absence. They often do so in a way that is improper, often by bullying, intimidation, or sheer brute force.

But not all Sheriffs are bad. Some families need a tough guy to stand up and get something done. A Sheriff may be just what a family needs if it is threatened by some outside force, for example litigation from an outside party. In other instances, there may be no other family member capable of taking over the responsibilities of a Patriarch.

Sheriffs' motivations vary. Some may be motivated by greed while others are motivated by compassion. Still others may be motivated by a sense of justice or by impatience.

If a Sheriff is acting improperly, there are a couple approaches the family can take. The hardline approach is to challenge the Sheriff directly. Generally, family members will be more successful at this if they band together and confront the Sheriff as a group. An alternative approach may be to simply reason with the Sheriff. Sheriffs can be short-sighted and they often fail to see other peoples' perspectives. For example, this might lead to a Sheriff's misconception that he is the only one available to take on the Patriarch's duties. Simply showing the Sheriff how those duties can be divided among the other family members may prove more effective than expected. Family members should never attempt to subvert a Sheriff by influencing the Patriarch behind the Sheriff's back. Getting Daddy to change his Will because Brother is a bully will surely lead to litigation.

3.6 Children & Grandchildren:

The relationship between grandparents and grandchildren can be very special. For many, a grandchild signifies success. The genes have been passed down far enough that we can feel relatively secure in their continuation. Grandchildren also give us hope and a sense of renewal. They present a second chance to get childrearing right. And don't forget the best part of all: When the grandkids are bad, grandparents can send them back to their parents!

On the other hand, relationships between grandparents and grandchildren can be strained. Generational differences and childhood experiences can lead to divergent world views, moral sensibilities, and work ethic. Two recurring archetypal personalities are associated with grandchildren. As with other archetypes, these can be mild or strong, but they present regularly enough to merit consideration by anyone who is Building their Castle. Each is described in the sections below.

3.6.1 The Uninitiated Generation.

One way to measure financial success is by the increase in the standard of living that future generations enjoy. Oftentimes, Bootstrap Patriarchs come from nothing, but are able to build up a family's wealth over time. Their children witness that buildup. They experience the Patriarch's toils firsthand, so they understand what it took to build the family's fortune. Usually, these children experience better lives growing up than the Patriarch. They may have been born just as the Patriarch was getting started, but they often attend better schools, accumulate more affluent networks of young friends, and want for less in life. Even as the Patriarch transitions from wealth creator to wealth distributor, he loses his perspective.

By the time the grandchildren are born, however, the Patriarch is often already well on his way to becoming a wealth distributor. The grandchild never witnessed the Patriarch's struggle or hustle. For obvious reasons, this reality can lead to misconceptions about the value of money and the amount most of us have to work to earn it. In addition to this, the grandchild often attends high-end schools where both the substantive material as well as the underlying values can be very different than those learned by the Patriarch. We call this the "**Uninitiated Generation.**"

The unfortunate result of all this can be disappointing for the Patriarch. The grandchild may appear lazy, politically radical, and egg-headed to the Patriarch. The grandchild may lack the street smarts the Patriarch values. Sometimes the effect of these differences is mild, but sometimes they can lead to animosity and outright hostility.

In many ways, the phenomenon of the Uninitiated Generation is a product of the Patriarch's success. The goal is to improve one's circumstances, and that necessarily means transferring out of the school of hard knocks. On the other hand, the education of both the children and the grandchildren may be a factor. Even though the child may have lived through the Patriarch's struggles, he may not have internalized them consciously. Thus, the memories remain impactful for him on a subconscious level, but they never get effectively communicated to the grandchildren.

The Uninitiated Generation is guided by both entitlement and idealism. Of these traits, the former is typically homegrown—after all, who wants to see their kids or grandkids suffer—and the latter is usually instilled over years of training at the hands of the best academia has to offer. The privilege of morality is only bestowed upon those who can afford it.

The Uninitiated Generation is also naively fearless. They have always been told they can accomplish anything they want, and the reality that this is often dangerously untrue, can be lost on them. They lack the pragmatism to understand the amount of work, time, and luck necessary to find success in life.

Addressing the Uninitiated Generation's proclivities requires work on several fronts by various parties. First and foremost, the Patriarch will need to get over some of his or her personal hang-ups. A top-notch education is invaluable, both substantively and because it opens doors for opportunity. But academia is a world where strange ideas can grow. If you are a Patriarch having difficulty getting over your grandchild's academic psychobabble and poppycock, try to learn to accept it, as least as much as is necessary to open a meaningful dialogue. Education is usually a net positive for your family. You don't have to agree with your grandkids to accept them. In case it slipped your mind, we call this "respect."

It's particularly important with the Uninitiated Generation that Patriarchs foster respect for themselves as well. But it is absolutely critical that this not be done by force or threats. A Patriarch should earn this respect. Beginning this process may be as simple as telling stories about times of hardship so the grandchild knows the Patriarch struggled just like everyone else does.

Similarly, develop meaningful and impactful family lore. Encourage your children to do the same with their children, starting at an early age. The grandchildren need to be aware of the family's experiences in a way that influences their world view.

Finally, put your grandchild in a tough or humbling position. And do so early. If you have a family company, let your grandchild work the mailroom, sweep the floors, or answer phones. If these are not options, encourage your grandchild to take on the kind of tough jobs you did when you were young. Not only can you bond over this, but you will also be teaching him the value of a dollar.

On the other hand, if you are a grandchild having trouble connecting with a grandparent, the mirror image of everything above can work for you. Accept your Patriarch's views for what they are without letting them get in the way of your relationship. Try to understand where your Patriarch came from and what it took to build your family's fortune. Even if your Patriarch didn't build the family fortune, consider what it took to keep the fortune intact. Find reasons to respect your Patriarch, not because he or she controls your family's money, but because he or she deserves it. Try to put yourself in a crucible so you can experience your own version of what your Patriarch went through before you were born. Finally, accept the advice your Patriarch has to offer. His years of wisdom are something you can and should use to your advantage.

3.6.2 The Skip Generation.

Sometimes, Patriarchs have very strong relationships with their grandchildren. These relationships can be even stronger than a Patriarch has with his or her own children. We refer to grandchildren in this scenario as the "**Skip Generation**."

The Skip Generation presents most commonly where the Patriarch is a Bootstrapper. In this situation, the Patriarch has worked hard to amass a fortune and, somehow, lost touch with his children. Perhaps the Patriarch simply didn't spend enough time with the children to make a stronger bond. Perhaps the pressures of building a business made him a hard or even cruel person. Perhaps generational differences got in the way. Whatever the reason, the Patriarch and the children don't see eye-to-eye.

But when grandkids start showing up, one or more of them may develop a very tight relationship with the Patriarch. Perhaps the Patriarch sees potential in the grandchild based on his personality. Perhaps the Patriarch is impressed with how the grandchild overcame some adversity, or with the grandchild's career path. Whatever the reason, the grandchild joins the Skip Generation when he develops a closer-than-normal relationship with the Patriarch. Patriarchs may shower grandchildren in the Skip Generation with responsibility and attention, often much to the chagrin of the middle generation. Thus, the mere existence of a Skip Generation grandchild can put a family at risk.

Members of the Skip Generation can have varying motivations, depending on their own personalities. There is no one archetype that tends to spawn Skip Generation grandchildren. Nonetheless, they do tend to have a few character traits in common: For one thing, Skip Generation grandchildren tend to be smart, or at least pragmatic. They understand where the family's bread is buttered and they respect that. They are also willing and able to make their own decisions. They may have grown up being told by their parents about how terrible the Patriarch was as a parent, but they are able to see through this. They are evidence-based thinkers and, having seen something that doesn't jibe with what they're told about the Patriarch's past, they make their own call. Finally, Skip Generation grandchildren tend to be high achievers, but not so much that they are able to fully break away from the Patriarch's orbit.

These characteristics add up to a core motivation centered around family, not so much in the sense of hearth and home, but rather in the sense of heritage and background. Keeping the family on its long-standing trajectory is a standard motivation for a Skip Generation grandchild. For this and other reasons, a Skip Generation grandchild may well deserve the responsibility that the Patriarch gives him. Often, bestowing this responsibility is motivation enough for these family members.

From the Patriarch's perspective, understanding the impact Skip Generation grandchildren have on the rest of the family is very important. Skip Generation grandchildren are often perceived as manipulative, cunning sycophants by their aunts and uncles, cousins, nieces and nephews, and even their parents. In some cases, these perceptions may even be accurate. But it is worth noting that most Patriarchs (particularly the Bootstrappers) didn't accumulate their wealth by being idiots. They can generally identify and manage talent, or at least they could at one time. In any event, the Patriarch should address these concerns openly with other family members, who will be motivated by jealousy and fear, which often lead to a Family Power Vacuum. Opening lines of communication and assuring these family members that their needs will be met often proves a valuable defense.

Similarly, grandchildren who find themselves in the Skip Generation should be mindful of their position and the feelings of others. They should expect some finger-pointing and proverbial saber rattling. But upon receiving any new responsibility from a Patriarch, Skip Generation grandchildren should quickly set a precedent for their own actions and attitudes. They should show that they can be relied upon to perform as expected. They must not only talk the talk. They must also affirmatively show that they can, in fact, walk the walk. This demonstration will go a long way to allay the concerns of other family members and further the family's overall objectives.

DEALING WITH DILEMMAS OF CONTINGENCY PLANNING

4.1 The Inevitable and the Not So Inevitable.

Studies have shown, one out of every one of us will eventually die. So will everyone any of us has ever known. Life is full of unpleasant realities. The problem is that none of us know when the end will come, how it will happen, how long it will take, or what might happen in the meantime. This path is laid down by the Fates, so the only thing we can do is plan as best we can for the various contingencies, because the Fates, if nothing else, are unpredictable.

But a given family does not go through crises all that often. Most of us will only be present at the death of a few close family members, and we might go our entire lives under the auspice of only two or three true Patriarchs. As a result, most people don't know where to start with their planning.

They lack the critical experience they need to plan effectively.

Unfortunately, the legal tools commonly deployed to deal with the problems of life's final stages are quite limited in their application. They focus primarily on the inevitability of death and the possibility of incapacity. When you die, you need some mechanism for distributing your assets. If you become incapacitated, you need a mechanism for both managing your assets and expending them in a way that makes you as comfortable as possible. But this is the limit where our legal system abruptly stops benefitting us.

The German philosopher, Frederick Nietzsche might have described our legal system as "**Apollonian**." Apollo was the Greek god of the sun. He symbolized light, reason, and clarity. Although far from perfect, the legal system strives to impose rationality and predictability on an otherwise chaotic existence. In more modern parlance, we describe the Apollonian mindset as being "left-brained."

In contrast, Dionysus was the god of wine, dance, celebration, chaos, and festivity. He symbolized passion, emotion, and freedom from boundaries. The "**Dionysian**" mindset might also be thought of as "right-brained." There is almost nothing right-brained or Dionysian about our Legal system.

With some notable exceptions, Apollonian thinking is a killer whereas Dionysian thinking is a creator. We may have a great idea for a new business (Dionysian) but fail to act on it after we have considered all the barriers to entry (Apollonian). Each of us was (hopefully) conceived in a Dionysian act of passion, and most of us will draw our last breath in the very Apollonian environment of a hospital room.

The Apollonian and Dionysian views represent a dichotomy in the human experience. Much like the Eastern philosophical concept of Yin and Yang, each of us needs the ability to view the world through both lenses to be fulfilled. Too much of either one will cause us to lose balance and perspective in life, resulting in chaos, which we experience as sorrow, misery, hate, and pain.

Most people believe the only tool we have to prepare for the inevitable is our Apollonian legal system. And while the legal system is important—you can't effectively Build your Castle without it—you also need to counterbalance the cold, harsh reality of your estate plan with something that injects a counter-balancing amount of emotion and creativity.

Building your Castle involves working on a level beyond that which the legal remedies are designed to address. Building your Castle means preparing your family members for a transition of power and giving them not only the legal authority to administer that change (Apollonian), but also the knowledge and motivation they will need to succeed with a peaceful transition (Dionysian).

The knowledge your family needs to Build its Castle cannot simply be written down in a Will or a Trust. Building your Castle means setting expectations for the whole family by developing and practicing contingency plans so that the entire family can spring into action when, not if, needed. You want all the family members to be on the same page, so it's important they all understand the plan before they need it. By practicing the plan, stress levels will be lower, and the family will be better situated to make rational decisions. In a sense, this is a lot like running a fire drill for your Castle.

Similarly, your family needs motivation to stave off the Family Power Vacuum. They need motivation to put your careful planning into effect. Ironically, they also need motivation to treat each other rationally when a family member dies or becomes incapacitated and emotions are running high.

This chapter describes some of the legal tools commonly used to address death and the incapacity that typically precedes it. It will provide clarity as to what these various tools are and how they work. As such, it will dispel some rumors and delve into the related issues that should be on your mind when you are preparing them. Keep in mind, however, that these legal tools are only part of the picture. Other chapters of this book address the additional elements of Building your Castle that will bring balance to the system once the legal issues are addressed.

4.2 Wills.

A "Will" (also referred to as a "last Will and testament") is a formal legal document providing instructions for settling the debts of an estate (everything from credit card debt to taxes) and then distributing the remaining assets. A Will must be properly executed to be valid. There are a number of formalities for Wills, and they must all be met for the Will to be proved up in court. If the formalities are not met, the Will should be deemed invalid and inoperative. In fact, Wills are considered so formal that many lawyers capitalize the w in the word *Will* to show due reverence and respect. It is, therefore, very important that Wills are prepared by competent professionals and properly executed. Most estate planning attorneys conduct Will execution ceremonies in their offices so they can control these details and make sure they're done right. When non-lawyers attempt to draft or execute their own Wills, they often leave something out or fail to respect the rules, resulting in unwanted legal difficulties. Also, certain circumstances in your life may require special attention beyond what you might find in an online form.

Importantly, Wills only address the inevitable. They are only effective upon death, so they are useless in dealing with the myriad circumstances a **"testator"** or **"testatrix"** (the person whose Will it is, depending on whether they are male or female) might experience in the period leading up to death.

So, what can you accomplish with a Will? Ultimately, of course, the objective is to get property to the right people, but the way this happens can be deceptively complex. Several of the primary concepts are discussed in the remainder of this section.

4.2.1 Disposition of Probate Property.

When a person makes a Will, he or she gets to decide where all the property that is subject to that Will goes. This pattern of distributions may or may not follow the applicable rules of descent and distribution which apply to all probate property not covered by the Will. A few states have mandatory rules about taking care of spouses or children, but by and large we are all free to do what we want with our assets when we die.

Often the default rules are not what we want for our family. These rules represent each state legislature's best guess as to how average people want their assets distributed when they die. But consider this: Families in the US have around 1.9 children. How many families do you know with 1.9 children? The point is that none of us is average. We each have different circumstances, and our estate planning should reflect this.

4.2.2 Executor Appointment.

One of the biggest decisions a testator must make is picking the executor. An executor stands in the shoes of a *decedent* (the person who died) and serves to wrap up any unfinished business that person may have had. Executors are tasked with three basic jobs: First, they must figure out exactly what the decedent's assets were. This is often harder than one might expect, and attorneys are typically needed to track down assets, discern separate property from community property, etc. Next, the executor settles outstanding debts. And finally, the executor distributes any remaining assets according to the terms of the Will. By allowing testators to name their executors, Wills provide testators with the ability to pick just the right person to close down their affairs after they die. This is generally a much better option than allowing a court to pick for them because the court is not acquainted with the family or the testator.

When appointing an executor, most Wills stipulate that he, she, or it (in the case of a corporate executor) will serve without bond in what most states call independent administration. Generally, an executor is required to file a bond to guard against various bad acts and mistakes that might deplete estate assets. However, a testator can waive this requirement by affirmatively stating as much in their Will. Similarly, testators can opt out of dependent administration by affirmatively requesting independent administration. Under dependent administration, a court will be significantly more involved in the probating of a Will. Where a person has gone to the trouble of naming the person who will represent him or her after he or she dies, this extra supervision (which is very expensive) is not normally needed.

The amount of overall involvement a probate court must have with regard to a particular estate depends on the state in which the probate happens. Some states' probate laws are relatively easy to navigate. Others are incredibly onerous. In those states, people go to great lengths to avoid probate altogether.

4.2.3 Manner of Disposition.

A Will also allows the testator to specify the manner in which property is disposed. By default, most dispositions are made outright, with no strings attached. But this is by no means mandatory. Sometimes strings can be attached. For example, you may want to give your fortune to your child so long as she remains clean and sober or at such time as she is able to obtain a college degree.

Stipulations can be troublesome, however. For example, as social norms change, they may be declared invalid as a matter of public policy. A testator cannot, for example, stipulate that a beneficiary may inherit only if he or she marries within a certain race. Similarly, enforcement is a significant issue. What does it mean to be clean and sober? Who is supposed to check on this? Is the beneficiary's word good enough?

Similarly, property may be given in parts to multiple people. A testator might, for example, give his wife the right to live in their home for the remainder of her life, but give his children from a previous marriage the remaining interest in the home.

Property can also be given in trust, in which case, the intended beneficiary will only be able to enjoy the property when certain conditions are met. Trusts can be deployed to serve a variety of functions, including some or all of the following:

- Protect against creditors
- Protect against divorcing spouses
- Limit tax exposure
- Encourage good behavior
- Keep assets in the family
- Preserve principal
- Protect spendthrifts from themselves
- Manage assets for minor and incapacitated people

As the list shows, trust planning can be applicable to a wide variety of common problems. These are so common, in fact, that many practitioners recommend them as a default estate planning mechanism. Section 4.3 below delves more deeply into trusts and their uses.

4.2.4 Exercise Powers of Appointment.

Many trusts grant someone (usually a beneficiary) the power to change the disposition of trust assets. Such a *power of appointment* can be used to address unforeseen circumstances. For example, Grant grandfather might provide in his Will that Bertha beneficiary will inherit property in trust when Grant dies. Upon Bertha's subsequent death, the trust assets will pass to new trusts benefitting grandchildren, Gertrude and Gretel, equally. But let's say that, sometime after Grant dies, Gretel marries a very wealthy man and no longer needs any inheritance from Grant. In this instance, Bertha might exercise her power of appointment to give Gertrude a larger share of the trust assets.

Powers of appointment are relevant in this section because they are frequently exercisable only by specific reference in the power-holder's Will. People who hold such a power should check to see what, if any, limitations apply to them. If a given trust beneficiary holds a testamentary power of appointment (that is, one that is exercisable by Will), then the beneficiary should assess several factors: First, should the power be exercised? This will involve an analysis of both personal and legal factors, including tax ramifications. Next, the beneficiary must determine exactly how the power should be exercised. For example, many powers of appointment require very specific language to be properly exercised. Where this is the case, a statement like, "I exercise my power of appointment from Trust X in favor of Suzie Q" will not be sufficient to effectively exercise the power.

The exercise of a power of appointment is not a disposition of probate property as described in Section 0 above because powers of appointment relate to trust property, which is not subject to probate.

4.3 Trusts.

We can divide trust planning into two branches. The first, which is discussed above, involves planning that someone does for someone else. Usually, this means a parent planning for children or other family members. When we set up trusts for someone else, a certain set of rules applies. These rules generally allow a "grantor" (the person setting up the trust) to attach various strings to trust property in order to achieve creditor protection, tax savings, and all sorts of other benefits.

The second branch of trust planning is generally more limited in value, but important nonetheless. It involves planning people do for themselves with trusts. People who establish trusts for their own benefit generally will not reap all of the benefits mentioned above (although there are some notable exceptions, such as the relatively new self-settled asset protections trusts offered by a handful of states). But there are still a few attainable benefits, each of which can be quite valuable in the right circumstances.

These trusts are usually called **"revocable living trusts"** (sometimes **"revocable management trusts"**). They are not designed for tax or other, more sophisticated purposes. But there are a few ways in which they can be used to great effect.

4.3.1 Probate Avoidance.

Probate is a creature of state law, and the process of going through probate varies greatly from state to state. In some jurisdictions, probate is no big deal, while in others, it can be very onerous. Some states streamline probate processes for simpler cases but impose more regulation and court control on more complex estates.

In states where it is particularly onerous, probate is to be avoided at nearly all costs. In these states, a revocable living trust is the primary estate planning vehicle. To the extent such a trust can be established during life and funded with the grantor's assets, probate can generally be bypassed entirely, saving significant time and money. To accomplish this goal, a trust does not need to be particularly complex or sophisticated, but the grantor does need to take the affirmative steps of both creating the trust and funding it by transferring his or her assets to it.

Even in states where probate is not particularly onerous, it may still be desirable to avoid the process. This may be a matter of cost, privacy, or many other factors. It may or may not be appropriate to avoid probate. Seek the advice of a good estate planning attorney who can provide competent guidance relevant to your particular circumstances.

4.3.2   Incapacity.

For many people, particularly in states where probate avoidance is not a high priority, the biggest benefit of a revocable living trust is that it is the ideal mechanism for transferring control of assets as incapacity approaches. Many Patriarchs, even those of relatively modest means, will establish a trust for their own benefit so that someday, someone else can take over and manage their assets. Consider the following hypothetical situation:

David Dad has passed away, leaving Mary Mother and Dana Daughter. Mary is slowing down and relies on Dana for more and more support around the house and help managing her affairs. On the advice of her attorney, Mary establishes the Mary Revocable Living Trust and transfers her assets into it. Mary appoints herself and Dana as co-trustees of the trust, with each having full authority to act on behalf of the trust unilaterally. Initially, Dana goes over to Mary's home every week or so to go through bills and take care of any business Mary might have. As time goes on, Dana becomes more and more involved in Mary's care. After a while, it gets too difficult for Mary to fill out her own checks, so Dana fills them out before she comes over and Mary just signs them. Eventually, even this stops and Dana pays all of Mary's bills out of the trust. In this manner, the transition of control over Mary's assets has passed smoothly over time to Dana. Of course, Mary needs to be of sound mind to establish the trust initially, but if she loses capacity after that, Dana is right there to take over any time.

As discussed in Section 4.4 below, trusts generally function better than durable powers of attorney because trustees hold legal title to trust property. When possible, people should strongly consider the use of a revocable living trust for this purpose.

4.3.3 Real Property in Another State.

States almost always exercise probate jurisdiction over real property located within their borders. Therefore, if a family owns property in a state other than the one they live in—for example, vacation property—it is frequently recommended that a trust be established to hold the out-of-state property and avoid a second probate in that other state.

4.3.4 Privacy and Security.

Revocable living trusts can also provide privacy, and therefore security, to wealthy families. Many, if not all, states require that an inventory of probate assets be filed with a court as part of the probate process, at least in certain circumstances. Generally, such an inventory is public record for anyone to see, and increasingly, these inventories are available online, so stalkers, friends and acquaintances, and anyone else can examine them without having to go down to a courthouse. Many families use revocable living trusts specifically to avoid these problems.

Similarly, where security is an issue, it is possible to own property through a trust to avoid potential targets being identified in public records, such as in the real estate or property tax records. In order to accomplish this effectively, the person being screened should not be the trustee of the trust at issue, but there are ways to mitigate this. For example, under some trust agreements, it may be possible to appoint a temporary trustee to take initial title to a parcel of real property. After the transfer is complete, the temporary trustee might resign, thereby reinstating the person being screened. When this happens, changing the real property records to reflect the change in trustee is generally not necessary.

4.3.5 Continuity of Business Management.

Where a family business is involved, trusts can be very helpful. Suppose, for example, that a family Patriarch owns 85% of the shares in a family business, and the children own the remaining 15%, all outright and free of trust. Suppose further that the Patriarch is the only officer of the company with check-writing authority, and that its bylaws require a majority vote of the shareholders to elect new officers. In such a scenario, the business may have a very difficult time staying afloat after the Patriarch's passing. The Patriarch's shares will be tied up in probate, which means nobody will be able to vote the shares for a period of months, even in a best-case scenario. Because nobody can vote the shares, it is impossible to elect a new officer to sign checks. Payroll can't be made, loans can't be serviced, and bills can't be paid. The business literally risks having the lights shut off because of poor planning.

On the other hand, if the Patriarch's shares had been held in a trust, there would be no need for probate, and the shares could be voted immediately. This continuity of asset management can literally mean the difference between life and death of a closely-held business, so it is often recommended that a family's business interests be tucked into a trust of some sort.

4.4 Durable Power of Attorney.

Many families will not set up a revocable management trust because they feel it is too costly and burdensome. If any planning is done at all, the Patriarch might have a "durable power of attorney" drawn up. In a durable power of attorney, a person (the "agent" or "attorney-in-fact") is named to manage the assets of an individual (the "principal"). The agent, under this arrangement, owes the principal a fiduciary duty and must keep the principal's best interests at heart when acting as agent.

Without realizing it, we make people our agent all the time. For example, if you give your credit card to your teenager and tell him to go to the store and buy some milk, you are appointing him as your agent. But, as a general rule, that relationship terminates when the principal loses capacity. The exception to this rule is a *durable* power of attorney, which survives the principal's incapacity. There are some hoops to jump through to make a power of attorney durable. Generally, the power of attorney needs to be written and usually must be witnessed or notarized.

Although it may seem very much like a trust from a practical perspective, the durable power of attorney is a far less effective tool for managing someone else's assets over the long term. Under a durable power of attorney, the agent manages assets that belong entirely to someone else. The agent merely steps in to act on the principal's behalf. Not so with a trust. A trustee holds legal title to trust assets, so the trustee actually owns those assets. Of course, the beneficiary gets the benefit of the assets, but they are technically owned by the trustee. This may seem like legal hair-splitting, but it is profoundly meaningful when dealing with third parties. A bank, for example, would generally rather not deal with a customer's agent under a durable power of attorney because the bank is still beholden to the customer. On the other hand, with a trust bank account, the bank owes no duty to the trust's beneficiaries. Its only duty is to the owner of the account, and that person is the trustee.

Powers of attorney are also subject to abuse. Stories abound of family members and others gaining control of people's assets through a power of attorney and then making off with the goods. And yet, they are a necessary estate planning tool. The keys are to name agents carefully and then communicate with the family about what is expected of them.

4.5 Guardianship.

Guardianship is sometimes referred to as a "nuclear option" in third-party care, and rightfully so. A major goal of contingency planning is avoiding guardianship. Guardianship is the process by which a court strips away the rights of an individual (called a "ward") and gives another person (a "guardian") authority to manage the ward's affairs. Guardianship is extremely expensive, embarrassingly public, and emotionally draining for all parties involved. Guardianship is also extremely onerous on the guardian because a court maintains supervisory authority throughout the guardianship (which may last decades) and is generally required to review financial information to verify that nothing has gone awry.

Unfortunately, though, guardianship is the only option for many people. When a person with no estate planning becomes incapacitated, guardianship is often the only mechanism by which someone can step in and manage the incapacitated person's affairs. People who are born with cognitive disabilities often end up in guardianship because they lack the capacity needed to do their own estate planning. Also, there are some instances where a guardianship is needed, notwithstanding the fact that good estate planning has been done.

Building a Castle means getting ahead of these problems before they arise. Too many of us assume that we're going to live to some ripe old age, have a heart attack and be dead before we hit the ground. This expectation is, at best, foolhardy. The Family Power Vacuum originates in crisis and thrives on chaos. Unfortunately, there is no preventing the crises. Every one of us is going to die, and many, if not most, of us will suffer incapacity before we do. By discussing the eminent crises with family before they occur, we can develop a plan of action and thereby mitigate the chaos. This is Building your Castle.

TIMING ISSUES

5.1   Chronos & Kairos.

The ancient Greeks had two very different concepts of time. The first was "**Chronos**." Chronos refers to linear time, quantitatively measurable in minutes and seconds. In modern English, we incorporate this notion in words like *chronological* and *chronometer*. Chronos is also the thing that kills us as it slowly wastes away. In more modern times, we have developed this idea into the concept of Father Time, who is often portrayed as a bearded old man with a scythe.

In contrast, the Greeks also acknowledged the concept of "**Kairos**" as a different form of time. Kairos was qualitative and could not be measured. It represented opportunity, or the right moment for something to happen. In some instances, Kairos also referred to the seasons. When we say, "Strike while the iron is hot," we're talking about Kairos.

In this chapter, we focus on Kairos. Building your Castle means recognizing and taking advantage of opportunities when they arise. It also means taking affirmative steps to create opportunities along the way. Most families simply accept the reality of Chronos—that time will march inevitably on—and leave it at that. Most families won't bother to recognize the opportunities that surround them, so they will not seize those opportunities. Moreover, very few families will ever put in the effort required to create opportunities. But if you do the work, it is possible to create your own opportunities and take advantage of them.

In the sections below, we will discuss how and when to take particular actions that are common to families that have successfully Built their Castle. The battle is always against Chronos because your time will eventually run out. If you don't do the things you need to do when you need to do them (Kairos), your Castle will never get Built.

5.2 Family Assemblies.

The Family Assembly is a key component of most successful families. Some families hold Assemblies regularly without realizing it. Through a fortuitous combination of family habits and personal traits, they stumble into traditions that achieve the same goals as the more formalized gatherings discussed in this book. This is not to say that these families achieve success unintentionally. Much to the contrary, in fact. But they do not set out with the deliberate purpose that is discussed in this book. If yours is one of these families, great! Keep doing what you're doing.

A Family Assembly is more than just a gathering of family members. To function as Family Assemblies, gatherings need to facilitate the amicable and cordial transfer of specific information with the purpose of establishing and furthering the family's goals. The exact information varies from family to family, but you generally need to cover family financial and business matters, contingency planning, grievances, the outlook and perspective of the enfranchised family members, and any ongoing issues requiring the special attention of one or more family members. Some families can cover all of these issues, at least inasmuch as they are relevant to their particular circumstances, without any formalized structure. Most families, however, adopt certain formalities to help ensure that their Family Assemblies are fruitful. Without a formal structure to keep the various family members on track and acting civilly towards one another, the family can run into problems. People get bored, so they stop paying attention. Tempers flare. Emotional baggage limits individuals' abilities to act rationally. Some people can get past these things on their own, and every now and then, each and every enfranchised member of a given family is just such a person, at least for a time. But this it is the exception, not the rule. The vast majority of us, on the other hand, are unable to hold successful and productive Family Assemblies spontaneously, so we have to go about making them happen.

The nuts and bolts of a Family Assembly are described in detail in Chapter 6, but two threshold issues must first be addressed: When will the first Family Assembly be held and how often will they be held moving forward. When considering these issues, there are just a few hard and fast rules, but it may help to think about the second question first.

Some families have their Assemblies weekly (Sunday dinner). Some families only have Assemblies every few years. Some families have mini-meetings every week with a major Assembly once a year. Some families have full-fledged Assemblies on a quarterly basis, and others stick to a looser schedule, meeting on an as-needed basis.

Much of this will be dictated by the dynamics of a given family. If the family is effectively a single nuclear group (a mother, a father, and one or more children), then more frequent meetings will be easily managed. If the family consists of several nuclear groups, then fewer meetings will likely be preferred. Similarly, some people like meetings more than others, and of course, this applies to Family Assemblies too. If certain family members only agree to participate in the Family Assemblies reluctantly, then you may wish to have fewer of them.

But Family Assemblies do need to be periodic and ongoing. Building your Castle takes work, and that work only ends when you die or become incapacitated. Life is fluid and dynamic. The world around us changes constantly, so we have to continually update ourselves with new information and constantly reevaluate our circumstances. Along the same vein, regrouping as a family periodically and assessing the progress individual family members have made on their particular tasks is important.

Thus, if there is one rule that governs the issue of when to have Family Assemblies, it is this: Have them regularly. We don't always realize it, but regularity has a subconsciously calming effect on people. It brings order to our personal universes. Regularity is certainty, and certainty uproots fear.

But regularity can mean different things to different people in different circumstances. One of the challenges all families face when Building their Castles is determining the pace at which the work will proceed. Families that cannot settle into a rhythm on their own should seek the counsel of a quality Facilitator for assistance.

A similar but much more delicate question is when to have a first Family Assembly. You might think that the advice in this book would be to begin having Family Assemblies right away, but this can be dangerous for two primary reasons. First, getting a Family Assembly organized takes a lot of legwork. Assume, for example, that a family wants to hold a two-day Assembly over a long weekend in a rural area about three hours' drive from their hometown. Even in this situation, a lot of legwork is required. Accommodations must be booked. Dining reservations must be made. Entertainment must be researched and paid for. And all of that is before any programming is put on the agenda. If a Facilitator assists with a Family Assembly, he or she will spend hours interviewing each attendee to understand his or her various personalities, goals, and outlooks. In short, Building your Castle takes time and preparation. You can't simply show up at a Family Assembly without a plan.

Second, even if you can work out all the planning, a Family Assembly will never get off the ground if the attendees aren't ready and willing to participate in good faith. For many families, one of the toughest obstacles to Building a Castle is getting everyone to buy into the process. You can't simply cram this down someone's throat. Many Patriarchs have learned the hard way that this realization must come from within. If a Patriarch simply invites all of the family on a vacation, then that's what people will expect. They will resent the Patriarch for springing something else on them without warning. Threats and ultimatums are similarly destructive. This is not to say that all enticements—even lavish ones, if that's appropriate to the family dynamic—are inappropriate *per se*. But until all the family members are ready to participate and reap the benefits, a Family Assembly is likely to do more harm than good.

The second rule of timing your Family Assemblies is that the first one should be held as soon as sufficient planning and preparation have been done and whenever all the requisite attendees, being fully informed, willingly agree to participate in the process. That may be next weekend, or it may be years from now. Each family will be different.

An ancillary rule—really a phenomenon—to the above is that it is easier to get younger family members to agree to participate than it is for older folk. Younger people generally have more to gain. They're also more optimistic about the future and more comfortable being told what to do. If children can be conditioned to meet regularly with their family, they will be more receptive to attending and participating in Family Assemblies down the road. As family members get older, accumulate more of their own assets, start their own families and careers, and generally develop more independence from the family unit, they become less willing to Build a Castle with someone else. For this reason, time is of the essence.

5.3 Enfranchisement.

Every Castle Builder needs to think about the enfranchisement of various family members. This is a Kairos moment. Enfranchisement, in this sense, refers to both providing someone with information and letting him be part of the decision-making process. In other words, when we talk about enfranchising a given family member, we're talking about giving him or her a seat at the table to both learn and participate.

Traditionally, enfranchisement has not been a concern because traditional Patriarchs don't normally talk about family business. Our culture tells us that it is inappropriate to talk about our wealth with anyone other than our lawyers, accountants, financial advisors, and other professionals who help us manage it. Because of these unwritten rules, many Patriarchs will not discuss their wealth with their children. Some won't even discuss their wealth with their own spouses. But the culture that makes us this way can backfire drastically.

Make no mistake, enfranchisement is going to happen. Eventually, something happens to every Patriarch, and someone else is forced to step in and take over. This may happen when the Patriarch dies, or it may happen when the Patriarch becomes disabled, but it's going to happen. This is the time when the Family Power Vacuum renders families most vulnerable of falling over the edge. It is an uncontrolled, fear-inducing environment that is ripe for disaster.

Building your Castle means avoiding this strain by taking control of the enfranchisement process. Fortunately, Patriarchs can exercise this control freely. Patriarchs who follow a set, transparent plan of enfranchisement will typically find that doing so reduces tensions within a family and leads to greater harmony.

Aside from the cultural taboo, there is only one drawback to family enfranchisement: It's very hard to put the genie back in the bottle. Once a family member has been enfranchised, it is quite difficult to take away his or her seat at the table. Besides this, however, there is no real disadvantage to the enfranchisement of family members in the business of the family.

Also, enfranchisement does not have to happen all at once. One important benefit of planned enfranchisement is that it offers Patriarchs the ability to monitor a family member after he has been given some minor responsibilities and thereby gauge when and how to expand those responsibilities over time.

Of course, families need not make their business known to the entire world. Enfranchisement is not recommended for everyone, and keeping family business private from distant family, friends, or strangers is still appropriate. But there are two categories of family members for whom the issue of enfranchisement is a little more delicate. These are children (and other descendants) and their spouses. Each of these groups is discussed below in detail.

5.3.1 Talking to Children About Money.

Enfranchisement involves two steps: First, you provide someone with information. Second, you empower that person to act on the information provided. With children, both of these steps are *per se* problems. Most people don't want to talk to their kids about money, particularly when the kids are young. But even those who have less difficulty talking to kids about money still have a lot of trouble handing over power to their kids as they transition through adulthood.

Let's start with the first step: The first thing to understand about kids and money is that they probably already know a lot more than most of us think. They may not have seen a balance sheet, but they are perfectly able to pick up on the signals of wealth we all project. They see the houses we live in, the cars we drive, and the clothes we wear. Even if our kids don't know the value of our assets, they can figure out the pecking order pretty easily. Also, kids can be more resourceful than we realize. Many parents are amazed when they learn their kids have looked up the value of their house and other assets online. In other words, children can be good at collecting data about their families' financial situation. But because they lack experience and context, they are usually unable to turn that data into meaningful information. It is, therefore, the family's job—and note that this duty may fall on the Patriarch or it may fall on someone else—to provide appropriate training in financial matters so the children become financially competent.

The modern view is that this process should begin at a very young age. Schools often teach children in the first or second grade to identify money and associate a number to each denomination. But they fail to provide the context of value associated with those numbers. Children of this age will often guess wildly at the cost of things. But you can help them understand relative value by making comparisons. Does a baseball cost more than a meal at your favorite restaurant? Does a car cost more than a month's rent? You get the picture. You can even make it into a game. When you go to the restaurant, have the children guess what the tab is. When you go to a grocery store, show the children the difference between the brand name items and the off-brand knock offs. Better yet, buy some of each and compare them subjectively. This is a great way to start conversation at the dinner table.

When it comes to discussing wealth with children, one of many parents' biggest fears is that the children will blabber to their friends. And of course, this could get back to the friends' parents and cause some awkwardness. This concern is perfectly legitimate. But games that teach the relative value of money do not raise this concern because they do not involve sensitive information. So, why not start early?

As kids grow up and discussions about money get more complex, some critical thinking will be in order. This step is one of the hardest in Building your Castle because it requires real introspection. Up to this point, the discussion has been on the financial value of money and other assets. But at some point, most Patriarchs want to interject moral values as well. How much consumption is too much? How much charitable giving is appropriate? What exactly is a steward of wealth? How should we treat those with significantly more or less wealth than we have?

This part of the process is particularly difficult for two reasons. First, even though we think we have a clear picture of what our financial morals are, we usually don't. If you don't believe that, you may want to take this simple challenge: 1) Write down the four worst things you, as a human being, can do to another human being. (Spoiler alert: You're probably going to write down something like *lie to, cheat on, steal from, kill*, and maybe one or two others.) 2) In the same amount of time that you spent writing down the items for step 1, write down just one financial moral. Most people can't do it. Why? Simple: Their financial morals aren't as clear as they thought they were. To be sure, we're brought up with social morals from the time we're young, but not so with financial morals, so we struggle to find examples that might guide us. Before most of us can effectively teach our kids to espouse to a certain set of financial morals, we have to develop those morals more fully in our own minds.

It takes work to develop these ideas, but they are vital to effective financial rearing of young ones. Since most of us don't even know where to start on this front, it may be helpful to seek the guidance of a Facilitator who can brainstorm and then hone these ideas down to a workable format. This may also be the focal point for a Family Assembly.

The second reason it's difficult to instill financial morality is simply a matter of optics. You have to walk the walk and practice what you preach. Children are observant by nature, and fairness is incredibly meaningful to them. If we tell them to be respectful of those who are less fortunate, but then fail to live by that rule ourselves, our kids will notice.

The best way out of this predicament is honesty. We have to be honest with ourselves about what our expectations really are and then model those expectations as best we can. If your teenager wants a nice car, you can't deny him on a theory of wanton consumption—"It's wrong to pay that much for a car!"—when you yourself drive a luxury vehicle. Instead, you'll have to find a different reason for the denial—"You can have a car like that when you've earned enough money for it yourself. In the meantime, here are the keys to something that will get you to school and back on time." The difference may seem subtle, but the psychological impact on your child can be enormous.

So, having an honest, heart-to-heart conversation with yourself (and probably your spouse too) before you delve too deeply into the realm of financial morality is important. Building your Castle means coming up with clear, concise rules of financial morality and then exemplifying them to your children and other family members.

Once you have made the leap to in-depth conversations with your children about wealth and the responsibilities it brings, a key focus will be making the subject not taboo, at least within the appropriate context of the family setting. A good way to do this is to simply talk about it regularly. Also, try to have conversations, not lectures. Talking down to your children will turn them off, but engaging them will turn them on so they are motivated to participate in the discussion. Seek out your kids' opinions and let them grapple with problems in their own minds. Let them work on tasks and do research on their own. All of this will foster the kind of team-mentality that lies at the heart of Building your Castle. And who knows, you might learn something in the process!

Speaking to children can and should be a rewarding endeavor. It should not feel taboo or icky. As our children mature, they will think more deeply about wealth and, hopefully, lead lives that are more enriched and prosperous for it.

However, many people reading this book will think they have missed the boat because their kids are already adults. If this is you, fear not, for all is not lost! Talking to children about money is a lifestyle that can begin at any time. Don't think of it like building a house without a foundation. Think of it more like changing your lifestyle to incorporate a healthier diet. You can do this at almost any time in your life and reap a tremendous benefit.

The worst thing a Patriarch can do is put off discussing money with his children indefinitely. This trap is easy to fall into. A structured plan for opening this dialogue is usually best, but don't put off the discussion simply because you failed to start it when your children were young. If you need help, hire a Facilitator, but do something to get the ball rolling.

Another point worth noting is that the principles of this section don't apply exclusively to children. Grandchildren also need to be brought into the fold, so why not apply these strategies with them?

5.3.2   Talking to Sons- and Daughters-In-Law About Money.

Children's spouses present a unique problem when it comes to family wealth. On the one hand, we want to foster healthy relationships within the family. On the other, we want to keep our wealth in the family. Balancing these two oppositional objectives has been a vexatious problem throughout human history. Each family is different (as is each spouse within a given family), and there is no single solution for each situation.

The good news is that there are a number of approaches available to families grappling with these issues. These range the gamut from complete exclusion, to default exclusion, to default inclusion, to complete inclusion. In other words, there is a spectrum of standards over which increasing inclusion applies. Also, there are two categories to which those standards can apply. The first can be thought of simply as family administrative activities. The second is wealth management.

Modern families are generally more willing to be inclusive in the family administrative activities category than they are in the wealth transfer category. Thus, a family might set up a Spouses' Committee but not permit spouses to vote at Family Assemblies (other than, perhaps, on behalf of their minor children). In this way, spouses can be involved with the family's activities, but not in a way that binds the other family members. If the family wishes to increase spousal participation, perhaps the chair of the Spouses' Committee can have a vote at the Family Assembly and represent the spouses. On the other hand, the same family might stipulate in its estate planning that spouses may not receive family assets through their estate planning, and that spouses are barred from partner or manager status in any family business entities. This is standard fare in estate planning as a protection against divorce. Most people do not want to be in business with their kids' ex-spouses, so families take affirmative steps to avoid this problem.

On the other hand, keep in mind that the above examples are by no means set in stone. Nor must they be applied across the board. The above rules could be default rules with exceptions made for some individual spouses on a case-by-case basis. To avoid animosity, create rules which, on their face, treat all spouses equally. For example, there might be a way for spouses to "earn" the right to vote at an assembly. Another idea is to differentiate based on each spouse's tenure in the family. As is often the case when Building your Castle, there are many ways to get across the goal line.

5.4   Talking to Patriarchs About Money.

You might be reading this book to learn about how to apply Castle-Building strategies in the context of a family of which you are not the Patriarch. If that is you, don't feel left out. There are more of you than there are Patriarchs! But you face a difficult challenge because you have to convince your Patriarch to begin a dialogue about wealth.

Unfortunately, there is no special trick to making this work. The information you want is the Patriarch's to give...or not. Building your Castle is hard work. Most people don't like doing hard work if they can avoid it, and your Patriarch might just be the kind of person who puts their head in the sand. Lots of them do.

There are, however, some helpful guidelines. First, let the Patriarch know that you're interested in opening the dialogue. Many people don't even think to ask for the things they want from others. But how else will the Patriarch know you're interested in the first place?

Before you tell the Patriarch you're interested in knowing more about the family finances, take a minute to think about what you're asking for. You want a meeting with the Patriarch to discuss the family assets, and how those assets are going to be managed in the future. You don't need an immediate accounting, so make that clear. Rather, what you would like the Patriarch to do is schedule a well-planned, business-like discourse to be held in the future. By being clear about your goal, you can reduce the stress on your Patriarch and improve your chances of getting the information you're after.

Before you ask for this meeting, consider your timing. For the most part, the timing rules described above in Section 5.2 relating to the first Family Assembly apply here as well. Sooner is typically better, but you must be sure you are adequately prepared. You must also pick an appropriate moment least likely to induce an emotionally irrational response.

Next, take some time to prepare your request. You want it to be well-considered, concise, clear, and complete. It may take a couple meetings to actually get the point across, and it's OK to be a little vague in the beginning. You might even want to bring some note cards. You will also have to consider whether you should make your request one-on-one to avoid ganging up, or in a group to appear unified. That will depend on the nature of the Patriarch.

In addition to simply letting the Patriarch know you want to open a dialogue about wealth, asking about it will signal it is an acceptable topic to discuss. This notion may not have occurred to the Patriarch. In this sense, the request alone may help break down barriers that prevented the Patriarch from opening up.

It may be helpful to ease into the idea of discussing wealth. You might broach the subject at an appropriate time, but be clear that it's not something that needs to be discussed right away. Give the Patriarch time to think about it. It's likely that he will need time to put together the appropriate information, so be clear that you understand this. It may help to set a deadline, but make sure that it's reasonably far off in the future. All of this will reduce stress on the Patriarch, thereby making it more likely that he will see the value of Castle Building.

The second most important rule is to avoid the appearance of entitlement. Even if you don't actually feel entitled, you might come across that way. Remember that the Patriarch's Castle is his to Build or not Build as he sees fit. It may be helpful to simply assume you're going to appear entitled and make plans to dampen this appearance as much as possible.

Finally, stress to the Patriarch the importance of involving all your family members in the Castle-Building process, which will set the stage for what's to come. A family cannot Build a Castle without the participation of all the family members. It just doesn't work. Castle Building does not require every family member to participate equally, but it does require every family member's participation because every family member needs to have skin in the game. And universal participation begins with universal dissemination of information.

5.5 Talking to Trustees About Money.

A different set of rules applies when the assets being discussed are held in trust because the taboos of unwritten social standards suddenly give way to very specific legal rules. Trustees have a duty to provide beneficiaries with information. A distinct subset of this duty is the duty to provide formal accountings to beneficiaries and other interested persons. Sometimes, a trustee is required to provide formal accountings on a regular basis. Other times, accountings are only required upon request.

The duty to provide information cannot be waived, although it can be minimized in some cases, depending on which state's law the trust operates under. Many rules generally applicable to trustees can be waived by specific language in a trust instrument. However, a provision in the trust instrument purporting to waive the trustee's duty to inform will generally be ineffective. This makes a lot of sense when you think about it. Beneficiaries need information to secure their rights. If the duty to inform were waivable, everyone would waive it because no trustee would be willing to serve otherwise. However, this would make it nearly impossible to enforce any trust because the beneficiaries of the trust would not know what's there.

But the duty to inform can be a double-edged sword. Formal accountings in particular are burdensome and quite expensive to prepare properly. A trustee will spend an inordinate amount of time preparing an accounting. Often the trustee's attorneys will be heavily involved in the preparation of the accounting, and the funds to pay for them come out of the trust.

Because accountings are so burdensome and also because an accounting demand can be perceived as an accusation of fraud, they tend to upset trustees. If a trustee has a method of retaliating against a beneficiary, accounting demands should only be made when they're really needed. Consider, for example, a situation where a trustee is also a beneficiary with a power of appointment over trust property. When another beneficiary demands an accounting, the trustee/beneficiary might exercise their power to effectively terminate the requesting beneficiary's interest.

Because accountings are so burdensome on trustees, statutory limitations are in place to prevent abuse. For example, a state statute might not require Trustees to provide accountings more often than annually. If this is the case, a beneficiary might be wise to time his or her accounting demand carefully. If the demand is made right before a suspect deal is closed, for example, it could be a whole year before the beneficiary will be able to get the details he or she is after.

If family assets are held in trust, the trustee is well advised to take information requests seriously. On the other hand, if a beneficiary is looking for information and not getting very far, the law may provide some options. But beneficiaries should nonetheless exercise caution when requesting information from trustees. Not only will this hurt them financially (because the trust assets will be used to pay the expense of preparing the accounting), it might also bring repercussions for their future inheritance.

5.6   When to cut the cord.

There is one other, very important timing issue that warrants discussion in this chapter, and that involves cutting ties with a family member. Sadly, some relationships are simply so sour that they become toxic for everyone involved. Family being family, this book generally advocates for giving individual family members wide latitude to be themselves. But sometimes the best thing to do is sever contact. Cutting the cord with a family member is a case-by-case decision. The circumstances of each individual case are usually too unique to effectively and productively compare to other cases.

There are a couple rules that are brighter than others. Most importantly, if an individual represents a credible, physical threat to your person or that of your children, you should probably discontinue contact. The same goes for anyone who is mentally abusive.

Some parents sever ties with children temporarily, attempting to teach them a lesson, but this is not advisable. Generally, the rule is that you only cut ties when you intend for it to be permanent. You must be willing and able to live with the decision in perpetuity. If things aren't that bad, severing ties is probably not the right choice, and you should seek other ways to address the situation. For example, a therapist or family mediator might be able to help. Or perhaps a Family Counsel could be useful.

In the context of familial interaction, knowing where to draw the line between emotionally charged behavior and true mental incapacity is very difficult. Obviously, if a person is mentally incapacitated, you treat him differently than you do someone who has his faculties and is just a jerk. The former continues to receive the love and adoration of the family while the latter does not. But many Patriarchs go an extra step. To the extent a family member's incapacity is self-inflicted (at least, in the eyes of the Patriarch), many Patriarchs put up barriers until the family member makes an effort to remedy the perceived malady. Thus, if the family member is an alcoholic, the Patriarch may sever contact until the family member enters rehab.

But this may be putting the cart before the horse. Building your Castle is about bringing the family together as a team so everyone can play some part, even a minor one. Obviously, you shouldn't let a family member with substance abuse problems manage your investment portfolio. But if you give him some task he or she is motivated to accomplish, you can make his or her life more meaningful and, possibly, help him to recovery in a way neither of you might have imagined. On the other hand, if a family member's substance abuse is so severe that it interferes significantly with your work or other familial relationships, then severing contact may be appropriate.

To the extent possible, severing contact should be universal throughout the family. The family should be all in on putting someone out before it happens. Failing to be on the same page on this issue can lead to factions within the family, and a house divided cannot stand for long.

Finally, it's worth noting that the opposite of love is not hate, it's indifference. Excommunicating a family member should never be an expression of hatred. It should be an affirmative decision to become indifferent. The family is, in effect, closing the Castle door on the excommunicated family member, raising the drawbridge, and declaring that it does not care what happens to him. This penalty is indeed harsh and should only be considered as a final option for the self-preservation of the family and its remaining members.

THE PROGRAM: A BLUEPRINT FOR YOUR FAMILY ASSEMBLY

6.1 The Cornerstone.

Family Assemblies are the centerpiece of most Castle-Building efforts. More than anything else, they are the place where the rubber meets the road. Although much work can and often does happen outside of the Family Assembly, the information sharing and decision making that happens there are a family's best weapons against the Family Power Vacuum.

As we have learned in the previous chapters of this book, Family Assemblies will differ substantially from family to family, based on the various circumstances at hand. But many families are at a complete loss as to where they should begin. Others may need some fresh ideas to make their existing system more effective. In either case, the following serves as a guide. Feel free to adopt this program *in toto*, or cherry-pick those elements which are most appropriate and helpful for your family. By design, this example is a generic Family Assembly program; at the end of this chapter, you will find some additional modules to consider adding to your own program.

6.2   Planning and Preparation.

Failing to plan is planning to fail. It may be cliché, but nothing could be truer about Family Assemblies. Preparation is the single most important key to success. I once knew a person who was upset her attempt at a Family Assembly hadn't gone off as well as she'd expected. When I asked what was on the agenda, the problem was immediately apparent. She told me that she didn't want an agenda because that was too stifling. Getting her family members to agree to attend the meeting in the first place was hard enough, even though it amounted to a free trip to a beautiful resort out of state. She said she just wanted to be in the woods and bond.

To the trained eye, this example is an obvious path to failure. What the woman wanted was for her family to come together organically. That's fair enough, but it's never going to just happen like that, especially when one family member is effectively ambushing the rest into compulsory family bonding. A Family Assembly is work, and it should be approached that way from all angles.

Facilitators understand better than just about anyone else how important it is to plan ahead of a Family Assembly. Of course, they don't know the family well enough to walk into an Assembly without researching each individual up front. Before facilitators can do their jobs, they have to get to know all the people in the family to learn about both their personalities and their circumstances. Usually they do this by interviewing family members over the phone.

If you're planning your own Family Assembly, your starting place is the agenda. The agenda for your Family Assembly serves several important purposes. It provides a guide so the family can stay on track. Most Family Assemblies are broken up into various modules which necessarily go in a certain order, so it is important each module fit into its allotted time. Without a Facilitator present, keeping to the schedule can be particularly difficult.

Next, the agenda lets everyone in the family (including you) know what to expect. This allows everyone to prepare their thoughts and questions with more specificity, and it also fosters a sense of calmness. If family members don't know what to expect, their natural fear of the unknown may lead to unwanted anxiety.

The agenda needs to be carefully planned to balance work and play in the time available. By breaking up the more demanding modules with other activities, the Assembly will be more productive.

Being conscious of other people's lifestyle and habits is also important. Remember, the point is not to change your family members or bend them to your will. Rather, you're trying to discover and develop your family members' strengths. Many Patriarchs are, by nature, early risers. Many of their family members are not. But if your attitude is, "Damnit, I'm paying for all this, so I can tell you about how much you're going to inherit from me," you're not Building your Castle. If you want people to wake up early in the morning, plan a fun event for that time slot. Go golfing, hunting, or on some other adventure that even the family teenagers will be interested in and wake up for. The same goes for food choice. If there are diabetics in your family, don't plan on having pasta at every meal. Of course, a healthy dose of reasonableness applies to all lifestyle accommodations. You don't want a single family member effectively hijacking the Family Assembly. Use your judgement, and do your best to reasonably accommodate others' habits. As much as possible, you want to do all of this without appearing judgmental.

Ask the other family members what they want to cover in the Family Assembly. This could really help guide the process. It may be a hard question at first because your family members may not know how to respond, but it will become easier as they get used to having Family Assemblies. If a request doesn't make the final agenda, be prepared to explain why. Submit the agenda to all your family members in time for them to review it and make comments. You don't want your Family Assembly to be rushed or have a tense feeling of urgency. If you need to set a deadline for getting the agenda out, do so. Even when they're completely arbitrary, deadlines are often the best way to encourage timeliness.

You may not be able to fit everything that needs to be planned out on an agenda. A good planner will anticipate questions that might arise from family members and have answers mapped out beforehand. A very good planner will visualize how he or she will let the other family members participate in the Family Assembly and avoid talking down to them. Finally, a great planner will expect the unexpected. He will remain cool and collected when things get dicey and have contingency plans for walking other family members off the ledge. There is nothing wrong with being emotional at a Family Assembly. You just want to make sure that the emotions are constructive rather than destructive. A great planner knows how to identify and leverage the former while mitigating the latter.

6.3 Comprehensive Family Assembly Program.

The method taught in this book breaks Family Assemblies down into separate modules. Each module is an item on the Family Assembly's agenda. What follows are some of the more common modules at regular Family Assemblies. Importantly, this program is geared towards families that meet 1-4 times per year for their Assemblies. Many families meet more regularly than this, and they do not need to go through each of the modules below each time they meet. This is not a hard and fast rule, but if your family comes together every week at the Sunday dinner table, then the communication dynamic in your particular case is very different from those families who are only able to meet annually. Reading about the modules below should nonetheless be helpful for families that meet more frequently because it serves as a checklist of topics to cover at some point during a given year.

6.3.1 Module 1: Discuss Family Lore.

The first module in the Family Assembly is a review of the family's narrative. This is the time when the family goes over its history and traditions. The idea here is to get everyone fired up about the family. What makes it unique? What makes it tick? What is the family origin story?

There are an infinite number of ways to organize the family lore module. Here are a few ideas:

- Simply hold a round-robin where each family member gets to tell a set number of stories about the family that are important to them.
- Allow family members to go "scatter shooting" where each person gets to speak up as little or as much as he or she likes as things occur to him or her.
- Keep a family diary or scrap book and read from it.
- Tell the family's history chronologically from an accepted starting point through to the present.
- Adopt a chant or song that tells the family history.
- Appoint a historian who is responsible for keeping the family story intact.
- Share family photos from the previous year or farther back.
- Have each family member randomly draw the name of another family member and tell that other family member's story.
- Discuss the specific language the family uses and why.
- Discuss the foods the family eats.
- Discuss the family's country or countries of origin.
- Let each family member describe any mannerisms, gestures, or phrases they have co-opted from another family member.

You get the idea. The point is to have as much fun as possible with this exercise. The focus should be on positive aspects of the family. Sad or distressing events should generally be avoided unless they are truly integral to the family's story and/or serve to show how some adversity was overcome. That said, do not underestimate the bonding power of a common struggle. Numerous studies show the number one thing that makes humans happy is overcoming adversity together. We are hardwired for this.

The family lore module is a great opportunity to observe and enfranchise family members. The Patriarch should not do much talking during this module. Rather, the Patriarch should take this opportunity to observe the others and assess both their aptitude and mental state. If one child struggles to say something nice about another child, an astute Patriarch will take note and be forewarned. By letting the other family members talk, the Patriarch instills confidence in them, as well as a sense of belonging. These are powerful buttresses against the Family Power Vacuum.

The family lore module is also a great opportunity to inform new spouses about the family. By knowing more about the family's history, spouses can engage more directly with the family, which in turn may stabilize relationships. Educating new spouses may also be important for the education of future family members. If a family member dies, his or her spouse may be the only one who is able to tell their children where they come from.

Perhaps most importantly, the family lore module sets the tone for the entire Family Assembly. By keeping things upbeat and positive here, the family will be more productive in the other modules.

6.3.2 Module 2: Review Family Mission Statement.

The first litmus test of how the family has fared since its last Family Assembly is the review of the Family Mission Statement. During this module, the Family Mission Statement is read and each family member is asked to reflect on whether he or she has lived up to the Family Mission Statement's vision.

This reflection is typically internal and deeply personal to each family member because only he or she really knows whether or not he or she has lived up to the Family Mission Statement. A Facilitator may or may not ask participants to discuss their thoughts openly.

During this module, someone should be appointed to speak about the Family Mission Statement itself. If the Family Mission Statement has some special history, it can be recited. If the Family Mission Statement has some complicated meaning, it can be examined. The point is to get the words out there so each family member has time to dwell on them.

This is a perfect opportunity to mix some ceremony and tradition into the Family Assembly. Ceremonies and traditions of all sorts exist for the primary purpose of bringing people together in a single moment to create a lasting imprint in the human subconscious. Remember Kairos from Chapter 5? Ceremonies are about creating moments of meaningful, qualitative time. It doesn't matter if you're getting married, taking communion, graduating from school, entering adulthood, or kissing under the mistletoe. The general purpose is the same: Do something meaningful together.

A ceremony in this module can take many forms. Perhaps you observe a moment of silence for each family member to reflect. Perhaps the youngest family member recites the Family Mission Statement and takes a few minutes to tell the rest of the family what those words mean to him. The content is less relevant than the practice itself, so be mindful of clever ways to build in something like this.

If there is open discussion of the family's performance relative to its Family Mission Statement, that discussion should be kept positive. There is no sense dwelling on past failures. Accentuating the successes will be far more productive moving forward because it will motivate family members to follow the guidance the Family Mission Statement provides.

This is also a good opportunity to indoctrinate spouses into the family's values and purpose. This ensures the spouses have the information they need to interact as best they can with the family members to whom they are married and their children. It also informs them of the facts and traditions you want them to pass down to future generations.

This module is NOT the appropriate time to discuss modifications to the Family Mission Statement. The opportunity for prospective thinking and planning comes in a later module. During this module, the point is to look back and measure successes.

If the Family Assembly is going to be longer than one day, this module may fit best at the end of the first day. It may take a while for people to arrive on the first day, so you might not get to the first module before the afternoon. Similarly, you may want to begin the day with something fun, like a round of golf, some trust exercises, or some other activity early on the first day. You may also want to add in one of the extra modules between the discussions of family lore and the Family Mission Statement. It's fine to have this discussion at the dinner table, but you don't want to have the discussion while people are distracted by their own meal or someone else's.

If you only have time for a one-day Family Assembly, or if alcohol is likely to be a problem, you may want to put the discussion of the Family Mission Statement in another time slot. Arrange the program so it fits your family's needs and keeps people comfortable.

You want the experience to be pleasant with as little stress as possible. If people are bored and feel like they're working too much, the results will suffer. In the context of litigation, it's well known that mediators will often do things to make the litigants (and their attorneys) uncomfortable. They do this to encourage the litigants to come to an agreement. In the context of the Family Assembly, you want to do just the opposite.

If time allows and there are no other constraints, putting the discussion of the Family Mission Statement towards the end of the day will allow your family to finish the day with a sense of accomplishment.

6.3.3 Module 3: Status Update.

When most people imagine a family meeting, the status update module is typically what they think of. Of course, a Family Assembly is far more than just a family meeting. But that doesn't mean the status update isn't important. Very much to the contrary! Just keep in mind that it may not be appropriate to rush into things. Other modules will have an analogous effect on the mind as stretching does before a workout.

The substance of the status update module consists primarily of one or more reports on the status of family affairs and future expectations. This will often be the point at which the Patriarch does the most talking as the family's assets and liabilities are described with appropriate specificity. An accurate description of the Patriarch's estate plan is also germane to this module and should be made in front of all relevant family members with complete transparency. The implications, tax and otherwise, of any estate planning techniques should also be explained to each expectant beneficiary so they can have clear expectations of what is to come and avoid being blindsided by confusing legal jargon and unintended consequences.

This module can be a bit overwhelming for Family Assembly attendees because there will be a lot of information for everyone to take in. If necessary, each component of this module can be turned into its own, stand-alone module. Scheduling breaks during this module may also be advisable, to the extent appropriate for your particular family's circumstances.

It may also be appropriate to invite professionals to participate in this module. They can attend in person, by telephone or videoconference, or they can prepare a memorandum for the family members to discuss during the meeting. In this manner, the estate planning attorney, accountant, or other family advisor can communicate relevant information to the family as a group, with complete transparency, and (hopefully) in plain English.

Giving the various family members the opportunity to ask questions may also prove fruitful. Not only will they likely learn something valuable, but their questions might prove enlightening to the Patriarch as well.

When discussing estate plans, Patriarchs should make sure to declare their intentions regarding how beneficiaries are to enjoy their inheritance and put them on notice of any restrictions on the use of property. Being clear about property that will be held in trust after the Patriarch's death can go a long way to reduce friction between beneficiaries and trustees. Thus, the Patriarch should state clearly whether future generations will enjoy the estate assets liberally, as a nest egg, or only as a safety cushion. The Patriarch should also be clear about the ability of spouses to benefit from the estate. Finally, there will almost always be tax-based restrictions placed on assets held in trust. These, along with any other restrictions—such as those promoting certain behaviors—should be made clear as well. Many beneficiaries, even well-educated ones, expect their standard of living to increase significantly when they inherit, but a Patriarch's estate plan may dampen the beneficial enjoyment of inherited property significantly. If this comes as a surprise, it can lead to a power struggle within the family.

Of course, end-of-life planning is ancillary to any discussion of estate planning. By setting out a plan before incapacity, Patriarchs and other family members can greatly reduce these burdens on loved ones. To this end, the status update module should include a discussion of i) the nature and extent of the care a family member might need, ii) the expected costs of that care and how they will be covered, as well as iii) how specific family members might participate in assisting with such care and the extent, if any, to which they should be compensated for their efforts.

The status update module of a Family Assembly may be the most difficult for the Patriarch. Discussing wealth remains extremely taboo in our society, and nobody wants to think about a slow decline towards the inevitable. However, in controlled circumstances, these discussions can literally save future generations from ruin, so it may be helpful to view openness as a lesser evil. One way to mitigate apprehension in this regard is to set clear expectations for confidentiality. That is, family members should be made to understand it is inappropriate to discuss family business outside of the family circle. Also, clear policies for when and how such information may be brought up with younger family members will likewise provide comfort. In any event, a balance must be drawn between the need to promote family unity and the desire to avoid embarrassment (or worse) if details are made public.

Keep in mind that the Family Assembly is a two-way street. Not only do family members need to be appraised of their general status, it's also important to set aside time for each family member to inform the rest of the participants of his or her own personal status. For smaller nuclear families, this information may already be known to the group, but as families grow larger and as children move away, it becomes increasingly important for each individual family member, or perhaps each family branch, to present his own update.

The key to family member updates is focusing on facts relevant to the family's business and thus germane to the Family Assembly. The focus should not be on births, deaths, trips, and whatnot. Rather, the focus should be on how each family member is faring in his job, personal goals for the coming year, plans for getting married, moving to a different company (or, especially starting one), desires for professional achievement, and plans for starting or growing a family, etc. Think of it this way: A family member who is contemplating a departure from her law firm to start a new practice will be in a very different mindset than another family member who is about to propose to his girlfriend.

These personal updates are even more important when a particular family member is caring for another, incapacitated family member. In this scenario, it is critical for everyone to understand the extent of the Caregiver's sacrifices. This communication may also lead the family to some solution or compromise that benefits everyone involved. For example, I once worked with a family caring for an elderly Patriarch through the early stages of dementia. In that case, the Caretaker was very stressed with all the demands of caring for the Patriarch. The Caretaker was going over to the Patriarch's home so much to prepare meals and clean the house that it was taking a significant toll on her personal and professional life. Nobody else in the family had realized how labor-intensive this work had become. But once the Caretaker updated the rest of the family, another family member spotted a potential solution. That family member had recently sent his youngest child off to college and no longer needed a full-time housekeeper. In fact, he was looking for a side gig for the housekeeper because, while he didn't want to get rid of her entirely, he did want to cut back her work hours. The solution was to share the housekeeper between the second family member and the Patriarch. In this manner, the Patriarch got better care, the Caretaker got some time back to focus on work and her personal life, the second family member got to reduce his housekeeper's hours without losing her entirely, and the housekeeper got to keep working for the family she had grown to love. This is just a small example of how communication facilitated by a Family Assembly can produce great benefits all-round. This is Building your Castle.

Personal status updates can also serve to provide a reality check. Left to our own devices, many of us can become intoxicated by our grandiose plans. Sometimes, these can be unreasonably risky or dangerous, or perhaps ill-timed, or even unripe. Often, the exercise of presenting these sorts of plans in open discussion leads us to finally see their foolhardy nature.

Sometimes, we need others to point it out to us. If a family can persuade one of their own to avoid going down such a path of personal or financial destruction, it is doing just as much good as it is when it supports a good idea.

Dissuading someone of an idea he or she incorrectly perceives as great is a delicate matter. Great care must be taken not to ostracize the family member or put him down. The family member who thinks he has a great idea may quickly feel attacked or suffer from wounded pride when the family, even with the best of intentions, tries to dissuade him from his plans. This is a good place for a Facilitator to step in. It may also make sense to withhold any criticism until after the rest of the family can convene and discuss ways to approach the errant family member as gently as possible.

6.3.4 Module 4: Set Goals.

Once the update is completed, the family can go about setting goals for the future. This part of the program may be tricky because family members may not understand what options are available or the extent to which their eventual achievement might be realistic. But this part can also be the most fun because it affords family members an opportunity to think creatively and plan with hope in their hearts about the future. The nature and extent of the particular goals will vary widely from family to family. A family's goals will likely change over time as well. To the extent there is a large family business, a stronger focus on business objectives will be needed. These might include some discussion of:

- Goals relating to growth
- Acquisition or divestiture of assets
- Employee matters (including hiring family members, spouses, or others)
- Development of new products or services
- Tax matters

Other families, however, might focus more attention on personal goals such as:

- Family members' education
- Identifying charitable beneficiaries to support
- Family members' personal goals (i.e. weight loss or writing a book)
- Family members' professional goals (i.e. a promotion or achieving a professional designation such as board certification)
- Setting standards for the care of elderly or disabled family members

Setting goals necessarily requires the family to assess its particular definition of success. Some measures of success can be objective. For example, determining an amount the family intends to give to charity may be straightforward. On the other hand, success may also manifest itself more as a path than a destination. That is, the continuance of educational goals or developing new familial relationships (i.e. through marriage or the birth of children) are more subjective.

For many families, charitable planning is an important discussion point. In addition to selecting one or more charities for the family to sponsor and the amounts it plans to give, the family should discuss how best to leverage its charitable giving for maximum benefit. For example, certain strategies might provide more overall tax benefit and others might result in more perks for the family. A quality Facilitator can be useful here, also. At the very least, someone with significant tax credentials should be consulted.

6.3.5 Module 5: Plan of Attack.

Once the goals have been laid out, the family can map out a path to success. Typically, they will do this by first brainstorming ideas for achieving their goals and then by developing (and memorializing) clear steps each family member will agree to take in furtherance of each goal.

There are a few keys to doing this effectively. First, larger tasks must be broken down into progressively smaller ones until they become realistically achievable for the individuals responsible for their completion. In this way, the creative gives way to the practical. Also, it is important that all family members are encouraged to avoid creating work for others. Some families have rules effectively stating that the person who mentions some new task should be in charge of seeing to it that the task, if adopted, is completed.

Second, avoiding disenfranchising any family member is very important. The input of all family members, once they meet stated criteria, should be valued and respected. While the tasks assigned to younger family members will be very different than those assigned to older family members, they should not be described in terms that portray relatively less value. For example, a family may choose to enfranchise children at age 16. At that age, however, the child's primary focus should be finishing high school with the best possible grades and beginning the next phase of life (be that military service, technical school, college, or something else). While young family members may work at the family business in the summer, they will not be responsible for the successful deployment of the new marketing push for the coming fall. Similarly, adult family members with diminished capacity or those who simply are not interested in participating in the family business should be provided with some opportunity to contribute, no matter how trivial their contributions might seem. The very essence of family is promoted by each individual's opportunity to contribute and his or her ability to "own" some task. No one should be marginalized.

Third, deadlines should be placed on each step of the plan. Like it or not, it is a reality of human nature that the road to hell is often paved with good intentions. A family will have done itself no good if it fails to implement its plan, however masterful it may have seemed when laid out. By providing deadlines, individual family members can be motivated to take the necessary steps towards realizing the family's stated goals. Of course, the deadlines (like the individual steps themselves) must be realistic. This may take several attempts to get right—that is, several years' worth of Family Assemblies—so families should not be put off if they don't get it right on the first try. Rather they should adjust their expectations accordingly. To the extent possible, individual family members should avoid criticism of others who missed their deadlines. Giving a family member less responsibility for the coming year because he or she failed to meet deadlines in the past is criticism enough for most. Other than that, the family should focus on positive reinforcement for jobs well done and not harp on failures.

6.3.6 Module 6: Take Stock.

After setting out the path towards achieving its goals, the family may wish to revisit operational documents and procedures and amend or adjust them as needed. Are the nepotism rules for the family business sill relevant and just? Does the constitution adequately address methods for resolving conflict? Does the policy for loaning money to family members need adjustment?

At this time, it's appropriate to revise the Family Mission Statement. If it is not functioning properly, a change may be necessary. Small tweaks are usually preferred to large overhauls because the Family Mission Statement should generally serve as a constant around which the family can both rally and assess itself. Changes to a Family Mission Statement can undermine the sense of strength projected by its Castle, so changes should only be made for good reason.

In a somewhat similar vein, appointments to the family council and any committees should be made at this time. Note that this may not be something all family members at the assembly participate in. Depending on the particular family's circumstances, this may be the exclusive purview of the family council. It just depends on the particular family circumstances at a given time.

6.3.7 Module 7: Celebrate.

The final agenda item for most Family Assemblies is to recognize a job well done by all. It can be hard work to map out the family's year (if that's your timeframe), so thanks and congratulations all round are in order, particularly if and to the extent the family has been able to conduct its business peacefully and on schedule. Building your Castle is hard work. Acknowledge that!

6.4 Additional Modules.

The modules above add up to a Family Assembly that is comprehensive, but also a little generic. One very nice thing about Family Assemblies, however, is that they are dynamic and can be molded to suit the particular circumstances at hand. Many families may wish to augment the program above with additional modules that are pertinent to them. What follows is a non-exclusive list of additional modules that families can pick and choose from when designing their own Family Assembly program.

6.4.1 Run Scenarios.

Hypothetical scenarios can be very helpful to families in a number of ways. First and foremost, they are highly effective at combatting both fear and ignorance. Fear is a family killer because it leads to irrational behavior. Ignorance can also lead to irrational behavior, usually because it induces fear. In the context of a power transfer, families want to avoid being blindsided as much as possible. By running scenarios, the members of your family will gain a better understanding of how to handle such a change. They will also have the opportunity to think through the process themselves and ask questions which may inform the Patriarch.

Hypothetical scenarios also help acclimate family members to the realities of life. Things change, people become incapacitated, and people die. In the same way that soldiers train by crawling under barbed wire while live rounds fly over their heads, hypothetical scenarios have a numbing effect on family members, enabling them to keep their wits about them when the real thing happens.

Perhaps the biggest problem with hypothetical scenarios is creating meaningfully specific storylines for discussion. Many of us have left informal, generally oral instructions to loved ones, but the purpose of this module is to take a deeper dive into these issues. Very specific facts should be presented for the family to deal with as a team. Since it can be hard for unpracticed individuals to come up with these facts, a Facilitator may be very important to a discussion involving hypothetical scenarios.

Possible questions on which a scenario module might be based include the following:

- What happens if [family member] dies first?

- What happens when [family member] becomes incapacitated and needs nursing care?
- What happens if the business (or some investment) fails?
- Under what conditions, if any, should [family member] be removed from life support, and what is the procedure for doing so?
- Who will take care of [dependent family member] when the family Patriarch becomes disabled?
- What happens if a family member develops a substance abuse problem, gets into debt, or goes through a divorce?
- What happens when family members fail to launch?
- What happens if someone gets kidnapped?
- What is the protocol for a major environmental or other disaster?
- What happens if [family member] fails to have any children?

As with some of the other modules above, hypothetical scenarios can also provide the Patriarch with useful information. Patriarchs are thus well-advised to be more observant during this exercise. If the family members don't react in a desired way, consider whether the instruction is faulty. If a family member becomes emotional during a practice run, consider how that person might act during the real thing. A Patriarch stands to gain some very valuable information during this module, and the opportunity should not be squandered.

6.4.2 Third Party Narrative.

One very helpful module that can be plugged into your Family Assembly is simply to allow others who have "been there and done that" to share their story. Hearing the personal story about what it was like to go through the death or incapacity of a loved one will often resonate with other family members. It will also have much of the same effect as running scenarios in that it will help family members accept reality and, hopefully, combat fear and ignorance.

If your family wants to present a third-party narrative, a few tips will be helpful. First, hear the story live and in person, so you can ask questions of the third party and get the full story. If it is too difficult to get the third-party to the particular venue where the Family Assembly is being held, then have them participate by phone or video conference. In a worst-case scenario, have a family member interview the third party and then report on his story. You don't want to prepare some sort of written narrative and ask the family members to read it. Most of them won't bother, and they won't get as much out of the experience if they don't engage with another human being.

Close family friends are the best candidates to talk about their stories. It also helps if they are not lawyers. Non-lawyers will be more credible, on the one hand, and they will speak in a vernacular that is more intelligible to the rest of the family.

6.4.3 Educational Modules.

Educational modules can also be very useful at a Family Assembly. The possible topics are endless and may include things like:

- Topics relevant to the family business
- Investment topics
- Tax issues
- Personal safety
- Market analysis
- Discussions of exotic assets like art, vacation property, aircraft, or boats.

The topics chosen can vary from year to year, but they will often be heavily influenced by the family's specific business and other activities. For example, if the family is focused on a particular business, then it may gravitate towards topics related to that business, but if the family's assets consist mainly of investments, then things like market analysis and tax trends might be more relevant.

For this module, the presenting expert may or may not be live. It is also possible to assign one family member to become an expert on the chosen topic and allow them to present the information. This is a great way to enfranchise young family members. Depending on the size of the family, educational modules can be scheduled as breakout sessions for family members to choose between. They can also be made available to fill time when certain family members, such as those on an executive committee, are busy with other business.

6.4.4 "Spotlight."

As the name implies, it may be appropriate to set time for a module in which a particular family member or group is spotlighted. This is just an opportunity to dig a little deeper into the life of a particular individual or family subgroup. It will be most useful where the family is spread out geographically and unable to gather as a group outside of the Family Assembly.

6.4.5 Kids' Presentation.

Small children can be a joy to watch, and it can be heartwarming to see them come together as a group for a small presentation to the other family members. A kids' presentation can be orchestrated by a spouse or other family member during earlier modules. It can also be as short or as long as the family desires.

6.4.6 Enfranchisement Ceremonies.

When a young family member or a spouse is enfranchised, some manner of pomp and circumstance is warranted. Something akin to being knighted by a king or queen, all the family members need to recognize it is a great honor to have a seat at the table. Therefore, some sort of formal and outward acknowledgment is appropriate when this happens.

Determining just what such a ceremony should look like will require a bit of creativity. Is some sort of oath required? What symbolism is appropriate? How long should it last? If enfranchisement is gradual, is a ceremony appropriate at every step? These and many other questions must be answered before a ceremony can be conceived, but the process of doing this can be quite fun.

6.4.7 Committee Meetings.

Large families will often have committees that carry out certain family business. Depending on the family dynamic, holding committee meetings at the Family Assembly may be appropriate. Of course, certain committees will necessarily need to meet sometime other than during the Family Assembly.

6.4.8 Grievance Hearings.

A good Family Constitution will provide mechanisms for addressing grievances among family members. Often, these will require some sort of hearing or arbitration by other family members. If a grievance is to be heard, time will need to be set aside at the Family Assembly for this purpose.

Grievance hearings can be pivotal for families because they both define and enforce what it means to be a part of the family. These are excellent teaching tools for younger generations and spouses. For these reasons, the grievance process should be as transparent as possible.

Where a significant grievance is present, however, care must be taken to avoid fracturing the family except in the most dire situations. A slighted individual can be incredibly disruptive to the rest of the family. Justice, as it were, should be meted out fairly and consistently, and once a decision is made, the family should not harp on it.

6.4.9 Planning Future Assemblies.

Depending on the family dynamic, Family Assemblies might be planned by a designated group or individual, or they might be planned by the family as a whole. In the latter case, a planning module for future Family Assemblies should be scheduled.

6.4.10 Elections.

Elections are also an important administrative part of some Family Assemblies. Smaller families may not elect any positions, but in larger families, particularly those with various committees, elections will be required. If elections are held privately, votes may be cast during breaks, but where elections are open, a separate module may be needed.

6.4.11 Family Photographs.

As with any reunion, Family Assemblies present a perfect opportunity to take photographs of the entire family together. This opportunity should not be squandered. Just make sure that everyone has been provided with relevant information outlining what to wear and any other important details.

6.4.12 Blind Evaluations.

For families that emphasize conformity, group evaluations may be effective. These might be carried out in many ways, but one of the most effective is the blind evaluation. In this model, each family member is excused from the designated meeting area for a period of time during which the remaining family members discuss the absentee's performance since the last Family Assembly and other characteristics. At the conclusion of this discussion, a scrivener prepares a short report, which all the remaining family members sign, such that the report constitutes the word of all of them. The absentee is then permitted to review the report. Although this may seem draconian, it doesn't need to be. With proper management, it can serve to motivate each individual family member and bolster family cohesion.

Often, ground rules are needed to maintain civility and harmony. For example, a family might stipulate that only positive feedback is allowed, or that it is only allowed in the absence of some extraordinary circumstance. Building your Castle generally focuses on positive reinforcement, so this option might be a little more in line with the other contents of this book. Some middle ground might be to allow only positive feedback in the report, regardless of what is discussed amongst the family.

Similarly, absolute secrecy is generally required from the persons conducting the evaluation. This promotes honest and open discourse between them.

Rules for the adoption of the written evaluation should also be considered. Must everyone agree to the exact words of the statement, or should a majority (or some supermajority) be sufficient to constitute the voice of the family? If the latter, should dissenting family members be allowed to present their opinions, and if so, should they be named?

Finally, families may or may not wish to allow family members to present rebuttals or pose questions after their evaluations. It may be necessary for each family to experiment with its rules until it lands upon a system that works well.

In any event, clear rules are required for a blind evaluation to function properly. It is critical that each family member understands and agrees to those rules before participating in the process. Thus, they should be written down in the family's constitution or, at the very least, its policies and procedures.

TIPS & TRICKS FROM THE TRENCHES

7.1 Flexibility.

Your plan for Building your Castle is just that, a plan. Murphy's law states that the best laid plans will fall apart. Despite your best efforts, things are going to get off track. The fact that a Family Assembly didn't go perfectly according to plan doesn't mean it was a mistake. Particularly in the early stages of Building your Castle, expect some problems to come up. Nobody Builds their Castle in a day.

Effective Castle Builders use the foibles to their advantage. For example, if the timeline for your Family Assembly proves grossly inadequate take note of that and schedule more appropriately for the next one. If one or more family members fails to respond the way you wanted them to, look for better motivations. You may also learn something about the family member himself.

Sometimes, foibles themselves turn into important family moments or memories. If someone says something funny or gets off track a little bit, that might become part of the family lore, or perhaps the family might adopt a funny tradition to prevent the foible from happening again. These types of things will strengthen the family bonds and help combat the Family Power Vacuum.

Addressing foibles calmly and rationally also demonstrates leadership acumen. Let's say a family member shows up at your family's annual Assembly having completely neglected an assignment he was given the previous year. The natural tendency is to get upset, but if you show calmness and restraint, other family members are likely to notice and respect you more.

7.2 Play the Long Ball.

Building your Castle is a process. It takes a lot of time and hard work to do it effectively. And once your Castle is built, it takes a lot of maintenance to keep it up. Don't expect honey and roses right away. Families are a long-term commitment. Treat them that way. Playing the long ball is about resisting temptation. It may seem convenient to do something now and reap a short-term gain without realizing or caring about the long-term consequences. Your Castle will be much more functional if you prioritize long-term goals.

7.3 Eyes on the Prize.

Losing sight of your real objectives is easy when you're Building your Castle. At the end of the day, you're trying to increase overall family happiness and wealth preservation through unity, shared experiences, and common values passed down from generation to generation. Keep that goal in mind as you proceed both strategically and intentionally through your Castle-Building endeavors.

Your strategy will play out differently, based on your role in the family. Even if you're the Patriarch, you don't Build a Castle for yourself; you Build your Castle for your descendants. Also, because it's impossible to Build your Castle alone, you will be forced to delegate tasks and accept your family members' work product. Getting bent out of shape over some detail that makes little or no difference in the long-run is not going to further your cause.

Conversely, if you are not your family's Patriarch, you should respect the Patriarch and support his leadership. Just as builders need a foreman, most families need a captain to lead them through life. The near-universal presence of patriarchy in human families proves its importance in family dynamics. We have literally evolved to understand that leadership from a single individual is generally superior to a more disbursed decision-making structure, even where that individual isn't perfect in each and every decision made. Family members would do well to remember this when they don't necessarily approve of their Patriarch's particular decisions.

7.4 Don't Keep Score.

It's easy to forget that every role is just as vital as the next, but this is a trap for the unwary, so every member of the family must be vigilant. Every contribution is valuable, and not everyone gets to be Mary or Joseph in the school Christmas pageant. The contributions each family member makes will vary in intensity, time commitment, and overall benefit to the family. Each person's ability and enthusiasm level is different. It is the duty of each family member to embrace these differences and accept the good-faith contributions of every other family member.

Exercising patience is often most stressful for Patriarchs. Patriarchs are often go-getters. They are proactive overachievers, and they measure success objectively. People with this mindset are often judgmental of anyone who doesn't at least strive for the same goals. For them, understanding that some people are simply motivated by other forces is very difficult. Also, the most successful Patriarchs often reserve judgement, at least outwardly. It's poor form for a Patriarch to pick on someone else in the family for failing to perform at an unrealistic level. But this often means the Patriarch cannot vent his frustrations to other family members, which induces stress. Finally, however, by necessity, the Patriarch constantly sits in judgment, at least inwardly, of all the other family members. It's the Patriarch's job to see to the long-term wellbeing of the family, which means that he needs to be able to identify which family members will be able to take on additional responsibilities and when. Because the Patriarch is waiting for other family members to grow into their more advanced roles, it is more frustrating to him when a family member falls short in some area.

In many ways, not keeping score is reminiscent of the feudal lord. Under the feudal system, it was the responsibility of each person to look after those below them. The lord of the manor didn't hire workers to fill a need as much as find work to suit the people under his care. That was a centerpiece of the contract of fealty. At least in theory.

Thus, the modern family that is Building a Castle deploys a similar mindset. Some family members will make objectively greater contributions than others, whether in terms of time, money, or some other metric. That's fine. What's important is that everyone has some avenue for contribution which is comfortable to them and meaningful to the other family members. Building a Castle is not a competition where family members are pitted against each other. Building a Castle is about putting up fortifications against the Family Power Vacuum. It doesn't matter how that wall gets built. The family member who piles on ten stones is just as important as the family member who piles on only one.

7.5   Fairness.

Make reasonable attempts to be fair but also manage expectations. The simple fact is that life isn't fair. We can try to make it fair, but at some point, the effort expended in the pursuit of fairness becomes more troublesome than the unfairness itself. In the legal world, we call this limit "reasonableness."

Consider, for example, the issues that arise around grandchildren. Wealthy people planning their estates are often vexed by the question of how to "fairly" treat their grandchildren. The issue is a simple one: grandchildren can be (and often are) born after a grandparent's death. Even without throwing death into the mix, gift tax rules can make it difficult to catch younger grandchildren up where previous gifts to other grandchildren have already been made.

It may be possible to provide in a Will or trust that equalizing distributions will be made to grandchildren who are alive at the time of the grandparent's death, but that's no help to grandkids who are born after the fact. Sometimes the numbers will not allow for a full catch up under any circumstances. Where equalizing gifts can be made, they may require such machinations in the estate plan that they become unreasonable. Therefore, the "most fair" option is to simply refrain from making any gifts to grandchildren at all. Of course, that doesn't sit well with many grandparents!

Where an underlying problem cannot be resolved reasonably and suitably, the next best thing is to manage the expectations of the family members. Patriarchs should make sure family members understand their intent in this regard. For example, if the plan is for a Patriarch's descendants to inherit his or her assets *per stirpes*, the branch of the family with five grandkids will have to divide the estate into more (smaller) shares than the branch with only one grandchild. The Family Power Vacuum is much more avoidable if everyone in the family knows about this fact before the Patriarch dies.

7.6 Live in Sin (to Avoid Blended Families).

We live in a modern world where consenting adults are no longer ostracized for being intimate. This social norm is one of many that has changed over time. What hasn't changed is the mandate of our human nature that the relationships between our children and their stepparents are, at best, strained. Even if all sides are able to put on a good show during a Patriarch's life, trouble almost always bubbles up when that Patriarch dies while married to someone who is not the other parent of the Patriarch's children. The problem is compounded when both the Patriarch and the spouse have children from a previous relationship.

Nearly all probate lawyers will agree on this: Nothing causes more probate litigation than blended families. But what is to be done? Most of us don't want to be alone. When life happens and we want to move on, it is far better to live in proverbial sin than to remarry and expose our families to the potential chaos caused by blended families.

Nontraditional relationships can be formalized through mechanisms such as domestic partnerships and cohabitation agreements. These are preferable to informal relationships which can result in miscommunication and unrealistic expectations. Formalized agreements can set out rights and responsibilities regarding real property, finances, family obligations, and many other factors. Under such an agreement, property can be held jointly or individually by each partner. The property can also be shared in a manner appropriate to the relationship. But by avoiding the legal entanglements of formal marriage, significant hassle can be avoided.

Note that this topic relates only to formal marriage. Commitment ceremonies and other, similar rituals or celebrations do not bring with them the legal entanglements of formal matrimony. Feel free to be as committed to your partner as you like, just don't subject your family to the legal nightmare of a blended family.

Note also that some states continue to recognize the concept of common law, or informal marriage. The laws of these states typically consider a couple to be married if they meet certain requirements. In other words, it is possible to be legally married in some states without going to the trouble of getting hitched in the traditional sense. Persons living in these states are well advised to take precautions that will prevent them from entering into such a relationship unwittingly.

7.7 Don't Give Up on Anyone.

It's easy to get stuck in your ways, to see the world in only black and while, and to believe that things don't change. The best Castle Builders resist these temptations. They find hope in every person and experience the world as a complex cacophony of ever-changing currents.

Like all good leaders, Patriarchs tend to be more successful when they find within themselves the capacity to build up those around them. This can be especially difficult in the context of family, where erratic emotions play havoc on the rational mind. But the simple fact is that people do change. Precipitating positive change in another person can sometimes require a swift kick in the pants, but sometimes it only requires a nudge. In either case, however, the person making the change was put on his path by another person. If we're not willing to help our own family members achieve their potential, who can they trust to help them get back on track?

As Theodore Levitt said, *"Experience comes from what we have done. Wisdom comes from what we have done badly."* In other words, we have all grown through and learned from our mistakes. Some of us can be more hard-headed in this regard than others. We all need to discourage in ourselves the desire to write off those who have tripped up more than we have. You never know how someone's life might change over time or how they might turn out in the end. Another way to look at this is that successful, productive people are the key to a successful Castle. You can't just kick someone out for no good reason, so the best thing you can do is try to turn them around and get them headed in the right direction.

In my legal practice, I have assisted many families as they tried, sometimes desperately and other times very lackadaisically, to get their children out of the downward spiral of substance abuse. Not only can this be ruinously expensive, but it is also an utterly maddening process. It usually takes something like seven tries before formal rehabilitation takes serious effect and shows lasting results. Addicts do things no rational person would ever consider. But if there is one unifying factor I have experienced time and time again with families in this situation, it's that success is most likely found where the family relentlessly works together in the belief that the addict will get better eventually. These families don't give up on their loved ones. They are willing to help their loved one get up no matter how many times he stumbles.

The same principle applies to many other conditions less severe than addiction. History is replete with examples of extremely intelligent people who struggled in school. Many highly successful businessmen and women struggled early on and only found their footing (and financial success) later on. The point is that family should never give up on family.

To be clear, setting reasonable boundaries and expectations is not the same as giving up on someone. Nor should a person be given more responsibility than is appropriate. No family member should be granted so much responsibility as to reasonably cause a significant hardship to other family members. But there are endless responsibilities that can be granted without fear of this happening.

7.8 Taking the Keys.

Taking an elderly family member's car keys away is never fun. It represents the end of an era and the decline of a loved one. While people can have good and bad days, or "moments of clarity" as some say, once the mind begins to falter, there is no recovery from the generally downward trend. Thus, the finality of the decline makes it especially dispiriting.

Of course, our elderly loved ones don't make the task easy on us. I once heard of a woman who simply refused to acknowledge her keys had been taken. Her family was concerned it would be too hard on her if they took her car away, so they tried hiding her keys, but she doggedly searched her house until she found them. Next, the family decided to keep the keys at a different house. This time, the woman called her long-time car salesman at the premier dealership where she had always bought her cars, and he, not knowing the extent of the woman's dementia, dutifully made a new set of keys and personally delivered them to her. The family only found out about this scheme when someone noticed that the woman's car kept getting more bumps and scratches. Eventually, the family had to take the car away entirely. They left a note by the front door reminding the woman that the car was at one of the children's houses so she wouldn't call the police. Not only was this experience traumatic to the woman, it was upsetting and burdensome to the family.

Very few of us spend any time thinking about, much less discussing with loved ones, what might happen when we are too mentally infirm to safely operate a motor vehicle. And yet, most of us plan to live long enough to reach this eventuality. It is therefore incumbent upon us to mitigate emotional heartache by planning ahead. Nothing can be gained by ignoring the problem. By discussing it openly, we stand to reap at least three significant benefits: First and foremost, we might save a life. Taking a person's keys is literally a matter of life and death. Not only is the elderly person at risk, but so is everyone else on the roads. By having a plan, we make it more likely we will successfully stop the person from driving before someone is hurt. Consider the woman in the example above. It is the nature of dementia that recent memories go first and older memories go later, so if that family had planned ahead of time, it is much more likely that the woman would have remembered the planning and not tried to drive.

Second, the family will be more unified. The default decision in nearly any context generally involves maintaining the *status quo*, if possible. In this context, the *status quo* is allowing the elderly family member to continue driving. If a family is divided as to whether the Patriarch's keys should be taken then the default will prevail, and the Patriarch will continue driving. If family members are unified in the decision to take the Patriarch's keys away, however, then the plan is much more likely to succeed. Unity is much more likely where a plan is in place.

Third, there is a similar unity vis-à-vis the elderly person themselves. If he has agreed to a time when his keys should be taken, he is more likely to comply. I once heard of a woman who loved to garden. As she got older and began to slow down, she told her children that when she could no longer garden, it would be time for them to take away her car keys. When the time came, the children all knew what to do, and they approached her about the keys. At first, the woman resisted. But when they reminded her of her own statement, she relented.

The trick with both of these unities is finding objective metrics that will function to signal that a person's keys should be taken at the right time. Not everyone is an avid gardener but perhaps some other hobby or activity can act as a stand-in. An experienced Facilitator can prove quite valuable in helping you hone in on a metric appropriate for your particular situation.

Some metrics do not function well. For example, specifying a particular age is probably not a good idea because there is no telling when a person's mind will go, and you don't want to take a person's keys prematurely. Nor do you want to take them too late. Many families take away their loved ones' keys when they have a car wreck (or sometimes several car wrecks within a short period of time). Obviously, this is a terrible idea, but it happens all the time.

The diagnosis of any of a range of maladies can signal it's time to take someone's keys. Anything that impacts the mind, consciousness, or voluntary motor movements should raise a red flag, as should any mind-altering medication.

There are also a few strategies for mitigating the impact of taking someone's keys. For example, giving up keys at nighttime only might be an easier pill to swallow than going full hog. Also, modern ride-sharing apps can make it easy for a person to maintain his freedom and mobility without actually getting behind a wheel. Creative solutions like this are worth discussing up front before the need to take a person's keys arises.

While the advice of this section is geared towards taking keys, analogous strategies apply at any time where there is a downturn in capacity. These might include decisions to move into an elder care facility, entering retirement, downsizing a house, retiring from the family business, or many other life events.

7.9 Rules of Family Decorum.

Sadly, our society has devalued decorum. Not that long ago, manners and etiquette meant something. Without them, a person's prospects were much diminished. Today, civility and politeness are most certainly out of fashion, but they remain useful tools to those who wish to use them. Indeed, it can be amazing how simple gestures will lighten the mood and maintain one's good graces. Some might say the family context is the last place where such frivolity matters; that one should be oneself, others' feelings be damned! But when Building your Castle, consider the opposite argument. Family should be the most important thing, so one should take more care to be courteous in that context than in any other. After all, you're stuck with your family members, so it may help to keep a few rules in mind:

7.9.1 The Golden Rule.

First and foremost, remember the golden rule: Do unto others as you would have them do unto you. If you're treating someone in a way that you wouldn't want to be treated, stop it. Instead, treat them the way you would want to be treated if your roles were reversed. Most of the time, this will engender happiness and goodwill. It can be hard to do—particularly in the emotionally-charged context of family—but the rewards are worth the effort.

7.9.2 Say "Thank You" (and Mean It).

When I was a boy, my mother was upset I would not thank her for taking me to and from school. I thought my mother was merely satisfying her responsibility as a parent. My thanks, I thought, should be reserved for extraordinary efforts. But a trusted family friend, upon hearing this, pointed out that it cost me nothing to thank my mother for a car ride. He also pointed out that it meant a lot to her and that staying in her good graces might pay dividends elsewhere. He then let me draw the conclusion that, from a standpoint of emotional economics, I would come out ahead if I changed my way. It felt awkward the first few times, but I have learned to thank people all the time for little things, even if they're just doing their job. And I'm much better off because of it.

The same principle applies in the family context. You will find it much easier to Build your Castle if you go out of your way to express common courtesies with your family members. This costs you nothing but may be very meaningful to those you interact with.

7.9.3 Lincoln's Unsent Letters.

In addition to his many well-written speeches, Abraham was famous for writing letters, many of which he never sent. When Lincoln was upset with someone—and he often was—he would write them a scathing letter. But wise as he was, Lincoln knew better than to send these letters right away. Instead, he put them in a special drawer in his desk overnight. The next morning, after he had cooled off, Lincoln revisited the letters. Some letters would be revised and sent. Others would not be sent at all. The lesson is that Lincoln had a system for addressing his anger so he came across much more tempered and respectable.

Castle Builders are well advised to take a page out of Lincoln's playbook and find ways to temper their own anger and other unproductive emotions. This is not an easy habit to develop. Lincoln had it easy. Email, smart phones, social media, and other methods of instantaneous communication were all still a long way off. The only way Lincoln could chastise most of his generals in the field was by letter. Today, we have many more temptations. Our culture also promotes instant gratification and rewards self-centered behavior much more than Lincoln's did.

But the lesson is sound. We all get wound up every now and then. The first trick is to pay attention to our own emotions so we realize when it happens to us. The next is having the mental fortitude to put ourselves on hold until the moment has passed.

There is nothing wrong with venting frustrations. Lincoln took the cathartic step of doing this on paper. This may work for some and not for others. The modern analogue to Lincoln's habit would be to draft an email and hold off on sending it. That is a fine strategy. Just make sure the email isn't sent prematurely by accident! It may be better to write the email without an addressee until you're sure you want to send it.

7.9.4 Atticus' Rule.

The last rule of family decorum comes from Atticus Finch in *To Kill a Mockingbird*. At one point in the novel, he famously tells his daughter, Scout, "You never really understand a person until you consider things from his point of view... until you climb into his skin and walk around in it." This is good advice if you are Building your Castle, too. There are an unknowable number of perspectives that you might be faced with along your Castle-Building journey. The better you are able to understand these perspectives, the better you will be able to address their problems and needs.

Do not be lulled into overconfidence on the assumption that you understand your family members' perspectives. This trap is perilous for the unwary. Indeed, most of us don't take the time to understand our own perspectives, so how should we magically understand those of our loved ones? Like most important things in life, we have to work at it. The various techniques discussed in this book will help hone the requisite understanding.

7.10 Crowd Surfing.

When it comes to the human psyche, compassion trumps defense. When faced with an accusation (whether perceived or actual), most of us tend to get defensive. This is a sure way to increase the tension in a Family Assembly or other setting. But the family setting is not the professional setting. When it comes to families, we should not fear litigation around every corner. We should feel comfortable trusting our family members to keep our best interests at heart. Thus, defensively explaining our failings and shortcomings can be counterproductive. Instead, Castle Builders rely on their family to accept them for who they are, so they acknowledge these characteristics in themselves without any need for forgiveness. This experience is much like crowd surfing because it calls on the individual to accept the support of the crowd for the euphoric and enlightening experience it is.

7.11 Have Fun.

Building your Castle is serious business. The Family Power Vacuum is a real danger to all of us. Don't put your head in the sand about it. Communicate with your family about the things that inevitably happen to all of us. If you need a facilitator to help you, find one. Also, take care to surround yourself with professionals who are effective and relatable. You need a working understanding of the tools they can bring to bear for your family's benefit so that you can effectively communicate with them about their work. Learn to identify who your family members are and how to communicate with them in a positive way. Find ways to let them help the family succeed, no matter how big or small their role might be. The goal is to approach this work rationally, and you will serve that goal best by minimizing your family member's fear and anger. Be thoughtful about when and how family members and their spouses should be enfranchised. Develop a plan for your Family Assemblies and start holding them.

Finally, and most importantly, have fun. Building your Castle should be your life's greatest work. Enjoy it. It's yours to relish. If you find the process isn't enjoyable, change it. Don't fall into the trap of feeling guilty about something you enjoy. Allow yourself the emotional freedom to savor the process and celebrate each and every accomplishment. This book provides the tools for accomplishing great things, and I truly hope you enjoy Building your Castle!

www.ingramcontent.com/pod-product-compliance
Lightning Source LLC
LaVergne TN
LVHW041630060526
838200LV00040B/1524